KNIGHTS OF MALTA

1. Tombs in St John's, Valetta, of the Grand Masters
Nicolas Cottoner (left) and Martin de Redin

KNIGHTS
OF
MALTA

A GALLERY OF PORTRAITS

———

CLAIRE ELIANE ENGEL

ROY PUBLISHERS, INC.
NEW YORK

39,834

PRINTED IN GREAT BRITAIN

PREFACE

WRITING about the Order of Malta at any period of its history takes the historian over practically virgin soil. However strange it may seem, very few writers have investigated the treasury of documents connected with this long Mediterranean story. The main collection is in the Royal Library of Malta in Valetta; about two-thirds of the archives are in Italian and one-third in French. There are also the Maltese documents in the Vatican Library in Rome, and the very important collection of the former Maltese Embassy to the Court of France, which is in the Archives Nationales in Paris.

In my bibliography I give a list of the sources I have used, knowing well that there are others. For instance, I have been neither to Vienna nor to Simancas. In France alone, documents about the Order of Malta can be found in the archives of any Department, in connection with the local Commanderies: there were 259 Commanderies in France, including Savoy, which came into the Langue d'Auvergne, but not including Alsace, which came into the Langue d'Allemagne. Moreover, every noble family has documents about ancestors who had joined the Order. Many documents disappeared during the French Revolution or the numerous invasions and ensuing destruction, but many have survived. I have been allowed to see some of them. Knights of Malta can be found everywhere.

I am fully conscious that my bibliography could have been more detailed. On the other hand, a fully analytical bibliography would have needed a great deal of space and I preferred to rely mostly on notes. I must refer my readers to my books in French, *L'Ordre de Malte en Méditerranée*, where the bibliography, not fully analytical either, fills ten pages of very small type.

This present book, and the two I wrote in French, on the history of the Order of Malta have taken me to many archives and libraries, and I have received the constant help and kindness of many scholars. I want to take this opportunity to thank them all, and mostly Baron Jacques Meurgey de Tupigny (former Curator of the Archives Nationales), M. Francis Roux-Devillas, Comte Gonzague de Monts de Savasse, M. Jean de Beaugourdon, Comte Jean de Bonneval, Signora Lanfredini,

M. André Chamson (member of the French Academy), Sir Hannibal Scicluna, Professor R. Halsband, Professor J. Godechot, Pastor H. de Cabrol, Messrs Leon Jéquier, F. & Y. Oltramare, Louis Evrard, Gordon Ruoff, E. S. de Beer, Roger Pierrot (Curator of the Bibliothèque Nationale), E. Taillemite (Archivist at the Archives Nationales), Noel Blakiston (Librarian at the Record Office), Gustave Vaucher (Director of the State Archives of Geneva), Depasquale (Head Librarian of the Royal Library of Malta), Miss Daphne Edmunds (Librarian of the Order of St John at St John's Gate, Clerkenwell), Dr Gutzwiller (Director of the State Archives of Fribourg), Dr P. Sjögren (Librarian of the University of Upsala), M. Aubertin, Commandant Vichaux (Musée de la Marine), and Mme Ducourtial (Musée de la Légion d'Honneur). Without their help I could never have found my way through an unbelievably intricate subject.

C.E.E.

Paris, 1962

ACKNOWLEDGMENTS

The author and publishers would like to thank the following people for their kind permission to reproduce the photographs in this book:

Dr Balducchino, 14b
British Museum, 5b, 14a
Central Office of Information, Malta, frontispiece
Mr Bredius, 13a
Baron Inguanez, Mdina, 10b
Baron J. Muergey de Tupigny, 9c, 12b
Library and Museum of the Order of St John, Clerkenwell, 7a, 13b
Malta Government Tourist Board, 11a
Musée de Grenoble, 9d
Musée de la Marine, Paris, 3, 4a, 4b, 5a, 6c
Musée de la Légion d'Honneur, 2a
Musée de Louvre, 8b, 15b
National Museum, Valetta, 9b, 11b, 12a
National Portrait Gallery, London, 9a
Royal Library, Malta, 2b

CONTENTS

ILLUSTRATIONS

CHAPTER I

THE ORDER IN MALTA

⤝❊⤞

WHEN the Crusades ended in 1291 with the loss of Acre, the last city of the Levant to fall to Islam, and the infidel tide surged to the shores of the Mediterranean, those who were left of the knightly orders sailed away and were forced to readjust themselves to new surroundings. The Knights Templar returned to France (their Grand Master had been killed during the last stand) and soon met a yet more tragic fate in their own land, where Philip the Fair suppressed the order so that he might seize its properties, tortured its members and burned them at the stake.

The Knights Hospitalier of St John of Jerusalem remained in the Middle East, first in Cyprus and afterwards in Rhodes, which they seized from the tottering Greek Empire. From about 1308 until 1522 the Knights held the island which thrust like a wedge into the side of the Turkish Empire. In this way an army, originally based upon the well-fortified castles it had built in Palestine and Syria, became a naval force and scoured the eastern Mediterranean in swift ships, always ready to pounce on a Turkish fleet. The ships remained a constant threat which the Turks tried hard to suppress. Rhodes was besieged in 1480, but the Turks were defeated and driven away by the Grand Master, Pierre d'Aubusson. They tried again in 1522, and this time they succeeded, in spite of the dogged courage of the Grand Master, Philipe de Villiers de l'Isle-Adam, and his knights. It has been suggested that the order was betrayed by a Portuguese knight, André d'Amaral, but this is rather doubtful; defeat, nevertheless, meant the end of a Latin presence in the Middle East. The Knights and most of the native Christian population of Rhodes left, and their conquerors allowed them to take their possessions, their weapons and their archives.

For seven years, the Knights of St John passed an anxious time in Europe, seeking a place where they could settle and continue their mission, free from eastern and also western interference. In a way, they dreaded western interference most.

The order, as a nursing order, had been founded shortly after the conquest of Jerusalem, which crowned the First Crusade. The Crusaders had quickly realized that sick pilgrims had to be cared for. Then it occurred to them that pilgrims must in any case be enabled to reach the goal of their pilgrimage safely; so the newly-founded Order of St John assumed military duties as well, in order to defend the roads that led to Jerusalem. As a knighthood, they acknowledged only the Pope as a spiritual head and their own elected Grand Master. Yet all the time, especially after they had been driven out of the Middle East, the Knights were not on very friendly terms with the papacy; this coolness, of course, was not outwardly visible, but Rome was always a little suspicious of a team of hardy adventurers which waged continuous war at the far end of the Mediterranean and acted as a sovereign, independent body.

Such opposition became more apparent after the Order had been driven west: the Pope kept them dangling for several years before offering them Viterbo to settle in. The city stood at the top of a hill, which made things rather awkward for a seafaring order. Then, as soon as Grand Master de l'Isle-Adam had accepted this unexciting gift, the plague broke out in Viterbo and the Knights had to leave in haste. De l'Isle-Adam tried hard to find some more propitious headquarters. There were negotiations in respect of Minorca, the Islands of Hyères, off the French coast, and Corfu; even the Isle of Wight was mentioned, though the beginning of the English Reformation made it a very doubtful prospect. Eventually, Charles V, as King of Aragon, offered Malta, Gozo and Tripoli. The main island was well situated and difficult to defend; Tripoli was hopeless, and in fact was quickly lost.

The Emperor's offer was accepted, as nothing better was likely to turn up. The agreement was signed on March 24, 1530, and the sealed Act is now in Valetta. It seems that the other copy, which should have been at Simancas, was lost before the eighteenth century. Villiers de l'Isle-Adam and his Knights landed at Il Borgo on October 25th.

It was probable that the Turks would pursue them to their new headquarters, and the Knights knew they would have to fight alone, since the European princes were hopelessly involved in their own problems. Francis I and Charles V were fighting in Italy, Henry VIII was intently watching what was happening on the Continent. This was the time when Luther, though he had been condemned at Worms, was becoming daily more powerful. No one cared for the Order, and its members knew that they could rely on none but themselves.

The Turks came, fought and were defeated. The new Grand Master, Jean de la Valette-Parisot, was both clever and courageous. Eventually a number of volunteers, mostly French, had come to the rescue of Malta, but the Spanish King, Philip II, and his Viceroy in Naples had done nothing until it was almost too late. After the victory the Viceroy was sacked. In 1566 Malta stood free, victorious and in ruins.

Then luck turned. La Valette undertook to repair the ruins and built a brand-new capital, to which he gave his name. Before he died in 1568 he had seen the first walls rise above ground in accordance with the plans laid out by his architect Girolamo Cassar. The Order gradually gained power and riches. It owned properties all over Catholic Europe; there were 259 commanderies in France, and more in Italy, Spain, Austria, Bavaria, the Rhineland, Poland and Flanders. True, those which were situated in the lands which had gone over to the Reformed churches had been lost, as in England, Scotland, Scandinavia, the Netherlands and Brandenburg.

In 1571 the Turks were crushed once more at Lepanto. The Order had sent three galleys to help Don John of Austria, the youthful admiral who had led the battle. These galleys had fared badly: one was captured and sixty Knights were killed. The man chosen by Don John to carry the tidings of victory to the Pope was a Knight of Malta, Louis de Crillon, who eventually became one of Henri IV's most trusted followers. Even in non-Catholic countries the fame of Malta was great. At the time of the Great Siege, prayers were said in the diocese of Norwich on Wednesdays and Fridays to ask for God's help for Christians fighting the infidels, and Queen

Elizabeth I ordered a thanksgiving service to be held at St Paul's when the island was relieved.

Then Malta started to lick its wounds and repair the damage. By the end of the century the Order had recovered its strength; it was rich, prosperous and covered with glory, and its fame abroad was great. Somewhere about 1618, Beaumont and Fletcher wrote *The Knight of Malta*. At that time, James I was trying to be friendly with Spain; consequently, one of the heroes of the play is a Spanish knight, Gomera, who saves and eventually marries the Grand Master's sister, Orinda, slandered by a felonious Knight who also attempts to betray the island. As the action takes place at the time of the siege, and as Jean de la Valette was about seventy years of age, Orinda de la Valette could not have been very young! But the playwrights were indifferent to such details, and were very vague, too, about the rules of the Order.

There was another Knight of Malta in Massinger's *Maid of Honour* (1632): Bertoldo. This time the dramatist knew the rules of the Order. Bertoldo is a man of daring and courage, defiant and unshaken in defeat, though less steady when fortune smiles on him; he reads Seneca in prison, but cannot remain unmoved when a beautiful princess, against whom he has fought, suddenly falls in love with him. There was more in Bertoldo's character than a dazzling part for a good actor; it gave a not unfair idea of what many Knights of Malta were like. They were heroes often; they never were saints. They were not expected to be monks or scholars, but sailors and warriors who could face death without flinching. The rules of the Order were strict, but many of them had fallen into disuse and the Order became a sort of aristocratic republic, bent on fighting the infidels in its own very independent way, resenting any interference from higher authority, not excluding the Pope himself.

Such an attitude became more and more obvious as years went by. Early in the eighteenth century, after victories at Malta and Lepanto, the Order had been reorganized and suddenly realized that its best days were over: victory had been so complete that the task of the Order was losing significance. By the middle of the eighteenth century there was hardly anything left to do.

Yet the Order retained its undiminished attraction and influence until the end of the Old Régime on the Continent. For at least a century any number of young noblemen joined it. Apart from a constantly dwindling minority who took their vows for religious reasons, they gravitated to Malta for rather mundane reasons. The Order provided younger sons of impoverished noble families with a pleasant life, which appealed to them more than a tame religious career, either as secular priests or monks. In Provence, where families were larger than elsewhere, it was not rare to find four or five brothers joining the Order. The Demandolx or the Castellanes sent any number of their sons to Malta. A Knight always had a very fair chance of becoming a Commander when he had served for five or six years, or when he had protectors powerful enough to put pressure on the Grand Master. Once he was a Commander,* the young man was out of the wood. He was provided with a fixed income which enabled him to escape the clutches of money-lenders, the bane of seventeenth- or eighteenth-century society. With luck he could hope to rise higher still, become a Bailly, be appointed one of the Order's Ambassadors, command a ship or a squadron, or eventually be elected Grand Master.

The Order held out great attractions for adventurous young men, and unlimited fighting at the time when it was becoming increasingly difficult to lead one's own private army on the Continent. Things were different in Malta: so long as the Turks were dangerous enemies, the Order attacked them incessantly from Gibraltar to the Dardanelles. This led to stupendous exploits. The high level of civilization had not tamed the bravery and daring of young men who succeeded in being polished courtiers as well as dauntless fighters. The old spirit of adventure was rampant among them, and sea battles provided them with opportunities to display audacity, hardiness, an utter scorn of death, and also their unruliness. Further, there may have been a more romantic motive, a sort of nostalgia for the days, already gone, when knights errant roamed the earth. There was a more or less secret romantic

---

* Commanders were given pensions out of the incomes paid by their 'Commanderies', their estates. The rest of the income went to pay various expenses of the Order.

trend among many men of the eighteenth century, for this was the time of the Gothic revival, of a passion for medieval lore and architecture, and Malta was consciously associated with the Crusades. The eight-pointed cross linked the present to the great ancestors who had lived in a picturesque and dramatic past.

In addition to those who sought to join the Order, Malta attracted volunteers too, who came for two or three years to learn the techniques of fighting at sea. Swedes and even Russians came for that purpose. The Order acted as a sort of naval school, whence sailors returned to serve in the navies of their own nations. The discipline on board the Order's ships was strict and exacting, but the officers were usually competent, action at sea was violent but well directed, and the Knights were provided with a fair opportunity for loot.

Young men—and older men too—could not exist on religious meditation alone: it was not even intended that they should do so. The Knights received a small pension only after ten years in the Order. Until then they had to live on the allowances grudgingly paid by their fathers, elder brothers or other relatives. Gambling was one of the plagues of Malta and the Knights were always heavily in debt. Young Knights who died at the hospital of the Order always stated in their wills that they owed money to their servants, tailors, bootmakers, various restaurants, confectioners, cafés and money-lenders. More often than not, they had pawned their watches and their crosses: one wonders how much—or how little—they could borrow on a cross of enamel and silver![1]

They therefore welcomed adventures which brought them good profit. They fought either in sailing ships or galleys of the Order, or as a team of four or five friends who together bought a ship, armed and manned her and waged their own private battles. They shared the profit, after paying a percentage to the Grand Master for permission to fly the flag of the Order. All this paid well, though risks were heavy; they usually boarded enemy ships. There was no point in running the risk of losing their prey by ramming or sinking it.

Yet, there was more to it than mere profit-making. They liked fighting for fighting's sake. All over the Mediterranean it was well known that Knights of Malta were dangerous adversaries. They were tough, well-trained men, more than willing to display their skill. Few things daunted or surprised them.

The life they lived in Malta may also explain the fiery temper of some of the Knights. The island is small, sterile and overpopulated. Even in the seventeenth century, large villages clustered closely round Valetta and the old capital on the hill, Mdina. Several Grand Masters built new towns, like Paula and Senglea, that were named after Antoine de Paule and Claude de la Sengle. Water in Malta is scarce and brackish. Alof de Wignacourt had parts of the island probed for water; some was found and a fine aqueduct was built to bring it to Valetta. Yet the water has a most unpleasant taste which makes it almost undrinkable. The lack of drinking water explains the large quantity of wine drunk by the Knights, which was imported from France and Italy, and paid for with olive oil.

On a small island, where everyone knows almost everyone else, tempers were easily frayed. It was difficult to escape from the far too familiar surroundings. There is little real country-side in Malta; apart from small orange groves round Rabat and Verdalla, some clusters of trees and caroub bushes, the island is a desert of stones and low prickly shrubs, affording a grudging shelter to a few hares and rabbits. One could go out and shoot them, and the Knights were excellent shots, but hunting to hounds was out of the question. Country houses could be erected in only a few places, and they did not provide their owners with the peace and privacy they sought. Beaches are few, which makes sea-bathing difficult. Most of the coast is a line of high, steep cliffs, some of them scooped out into tiny *calanques* similar to the secluded bays found between Marseille and Cassis. On the whole, life in Malta was not made to soothe fiery tempers. Hence the great number of quarrels that broke out between the Knights who were quick to draw their swords. Life was lively, perhaps too lively.

One of the unexpected aspects of the Order of Malta is that, without much, or even any, specialized education, Knights were called upon to act, not only as sailors or soldiers, but also as ambassadors, judges, administrators, financiers, anything. They usually displayed talent and fulfilled their tasks well. Was it because 'men of quality know everything without study', to quote Molière's Mascarille, or because they could improvise well?

On the other hand, the Order's political undertakings were not always happy. In the seventeenth century, the Order bought three small islands in the French West Indies, but panicked at the thought of the trouble those far-away territories could produce; they were promptly sold back to France. Later, Grand Master Pinto de Fonseca tried to claim Corsica for the Order, just when the island had revolted against Genoa and everybody—England, France and Genoa, not to mention Boswell and Jean-Jacques Rousseau—had a finger in that scalding pie. Pinto was both clever and ambitious: he had been the first Grand Master to assume the closed regal crown and the title of Most Eminent Highness. At the time of the Corsican affair, he applied right and left, publishing innumerable tracts to explain—not very clearly—why Corsica must and should belong to Malta. It went on until the French Prime Minister, the Duc de Choiseul, advised him to stop.[2] No Grand Master could defy such an order, for two-thirds of the Knights were French and the only sovereign on whom the Order could rely with any certainty was the King of France; so Pinto desisted gracefully.

Knights of Malta were scattered all over the world, for in the intervals between visits to the island to claim preferment or some new dignity they served their own sovereigns in the army and navy, or as diplomats and court dignitaries. They usually wrote to the Grand Master to give him detailed accounts of their new appointments, and the Order was therefore probably one of the best-informed states in Europe.

Above all the Order was not conventional. Grand Masters were often broad-minded at a time when few people were. Jean de la Valette had set an example so striking that not many realized how far it went. Among the few people who cared to help the Order when it was in deadly peril in 1565 were 300 French noblemen who went to Malta as volunteers; it was no fault of theirs that they arrived late, when the Turks had already abandoned hope of conquering the island and were just looking for a good excuse for re-embarking without losing face. This was given them by the landing at Mellija of the French volunteers backed by some Spanish troops. La Valette went out of his way to show his gratitude to the French, and to be extremely cold towards the Spaniards. Now, among the French noblemen were about fifty Protestants, members of some of the noblest families in France. La Valette, whose nephew, Charles du Puy-Montbrun, was an eminent member of the Protestant party, made no distinction between them and their Catholic colleagues. The whole episode has been surprisingly ignored by the historians of the Order, though there is a first-hand account by Brantôme, a member of that hardy little army and a personal friend of several of the Protestants, the two brothers de Clermont d'Amboise among them. This revival of the crusading spirit in the middle of the Wars of Religion is most striking. Several of La Valette's successors were similarly broad-minded. One of them, Pinto de Fonseca, in 1762, came very near to an oecumenical conception of the Order of the Hospitaliers of St John. It is a very intricate story.

In the fourteenth century, a group of knights, several of whom were Germans from Brandenburg, rebelled against the tyranny of a Grand Master. This was neither unprecedented nor sacrilegious at a time when there were usually two, and sometimes three, Popes competing for the mastery of the Holy See. The seceding Knights left Rhodes and retired to Brandenburg, where they elected their own leader as *Herrenmeister*. The Order saw nothing final in that gesture. After arduous negotiations the German Knights went back to the Rhodian fold in 1362, having been granted the right to elect their *Herrenmeister*, provided he was approved by the Grand Prior of Germany.

When the Reformation took place in Germany, things again became vague and chaotic. What was at first a trend of thought took time to ripen into a social and geographical situation. Two Commanders of the Bailliwick of Brandenburg adopted the new faith and married. The Grand Master was Juan d'Homedes, a rather shady character, loathed by most of his Knights. He took fright, wondering what would happen to the Commanderies. The *Herrenmeister*, Joachim von Arnim, paid homage to the secular Protestant Duke of Brandenburg. During the years that followed, thirteen Commanderies went over to the Reformed Church. It took two treaties, those of Augsburg and Westphalia, and over a century to settle the matter. The Great Bailliwick of Brandenburg bought itself free from Malta, while religious and personal connections were left to the Grand Master's and the *Herrenmeister*'s discretion.

Things continued thus for about a century, but in 1755 the King of Prussia, Frederick II, started negotiating with the Order about the Silesian Commanderies he had seized while taking the province from Austria. A few years later, in 1762, the King's brother, Augustus Ferdinand of Prussia, was elected as *Herrenmeister*. The King sent an envoy to the Grand Priory of Germany to ask for confirmation of the Prince's election and to settle finally the question of the financial relations of the two Orders. The Grand Master was Pinto, who was always short of money and was for a policy of prestige, while seeking the philosophers' stone—an expensive hobby. Frederick II's request was a godsend. It is also possible—but less likely—that Pinto understood how important would be a reunion of the two branches of the Order. It would bridge a spiritual gap, increase the power of both branches and the Grand Master's prestige. He consequently accepted Frederick's proposals, recognized his brother and sent a decoration to the latter's wife. It might have led to important developments, had not the Order already lost much of its power.

Daring is the word that seems to summarize the Order's virtues and also its vices. Most of the Knights did not conform to the period's moral or political code. They had strongly-developed personalities and they lived far from their family surroundings. There was no one to restrain them, as they scarcely accepted the Grand Master's advice or criticism. That accounts for the highly-coloured portrait gallery the Order of Malta displays to those who are interested in its history.

CHAPTER II

FROM MALTA TO SCOTLAND
NICOLAS DE VILLEGAGNON

֍

THE sixteenth century was a period of clashing religious loyalties. Men and women were unhesitatingly true to their faiths, even unto death. The various attempts to eradicate the Reformed churches engulfed Europe in a sea of blood, and martyrs went to the block or to the stake in ever-growing numbers. On the other hand, during that stern, devout, even fanatical era there lived a good many men who managed to use religion to further their own worldly purposes, though such an attitude could be extremely dangerous and required as much courage as a more dignified one. One of those ingenious people was a Knight of Malta, Nicolas de Villegagnon.

He was born in 1510 in Provins, in the Ile-de-France, of an old aristocratic family. He was a hardy, well-built, handsome child, who at a very early age evinced great intelligence and a passion for learning. Consequently, as the Villegagnons were a large family and Nicolas had a number of elder brothers, it was decided that he should study law. When he was eighteen he was sent to the University of Orleans to read for his degree. There he met Calvin, who was a law student too. They came more or less from the same part of France, for Calvin was born in Noyon in Picardy. They were to some extent in sympathy, though they were of widely different temperament. Calvin, at that time, was a slender, good-looking youth, with large fiery eyes and a short dark beard; he was an outstanding scholar, already intent on the graver side of learning and a follower of the new faith. After a year in Orleans, he passed his degree and left for Bourges; but Villegagnon stayed in Orleans, and it was probably there that he acquired his perfect Latin style.

A few months later he was involved in a very noisy student brawl, at which the authorities were very angry; he was expelled and had to leave the university without taking his degree. He was then about twenty and obviously thought that being sent down was not a really serious matter. He abandoned the idea of becoming a lawyer and got himself accepted into the Order of Malta, having all the required quarters of nobility. In 1531 he left for the island.

The Order had just moved in, licking its wounds after the loss of Rhodes and nine years of aimless wanderings in an attempt to find a place to stay, free from princely interferences, and free to carry out its task. Charles V, as King of Aragon, a title which made him suzerain lord of Southern Italy, had finally given them Malta, Gozo and far-away Tripoli, advanced posts of Christendom in the Mediterranean. They were very difficult to defend and the enemy was likely to strike at them at any moment. Villegagnon was a welcome addition to a team of hardy men on whom the Grand Master could rely at such a moment. This new life suited Villegagnon; he felt much happier in the lively, colourful, violent setting of Malta than in a small university town, reading law in Latin. He was a good scholar, but he was many other things besides, and something of an adventurer.

We do not know how long he stayed in Malta. In 1542 he was in Venice, on his way to Hungary, where he fought against the Turks. Then he went back to France for a few months and, as an officer in the Royal Army, he saw service in Piedmont. In 1544 he was back in Malta, and at that time the Order was more or less tied to Spain, as Charles V, now Emperor, had given them the island. Charles was contemplating an attack upon the Turkish regencies in North Africa. He asked for the Order's help, which could not be withheld, and they generously sent him four ships and 400 men. The expedition was directed against Algiers and it was carelessly planned and organized. It started too late, and it was the end of October—a stormy month in the Mediterranean—when the fleet reached Algiers, delayed by a succession of gales. The landing was difficult and the Arabs left no breathing space to the Christian troops. The Malta squadron fought them back step by step, and Charles V succeeded in placing his camp on the road leading to El Biar, a spot which still bears the name of Fort l'Empereur. Twenty-five Knights of Malta were killed during the fight, one of whom was the standard-bearer, Pons de Savignac. Villegagnon was badly wounded after having distinguished himself in the fight. In the end, defeat could not be averted, and the Emperor and his troops were compelled to re-embark. The return voyage was very rough, and of the four Malta ships three were badly damaged before they reached the island.

Villegagnon did not return to Malta; he pushed north to Rome, possibly to see better doctors, but also to be free to say all he wished about the unpleasant episode through which he had just lived. Malta was ablaze with anger and the Knights openly blamed the Grand Master for the failure of the expedition. They accused him of having kept for himself the money he should have spent on equipment, and of having been incredibly careless when arming his ships. Being out of reach of the Grand Master d'Homedes, Villegagnon was even more violent. In a long Latin letter to Cardinal du Bellay, the French Ambassador, he told a tale of murderous stupidity in which d'Homedes's mistakes were almost criminal. After such a display of cold hatred, upheld by carefully marshalled arguments, Malta was scarcely the place for Villegagnon to live in peace. His letter was widely read and Villegagnon was probably well advised when he left Rome, not for Malta, but for Paris. King Francis I welcomed him with open arms.

A few years elapsed and Nicolas de Villegagnon saw service again in very different surroundings. He was sent to Scotland. James V had died in 1542, a few days after the birth of Mary, his heiress, in Linlithgow Castle. The Queen Regent, Marie de Guise, was a young woman of great beauty, as stubborn, brave and ambitious as her brothers, the Lorraine princes who were to plunge France into a welter of blood during the years to come. Marie was contemplating the great diplomatic achievement: she was planning the betrothal of the baby Queen to the infant Dauphin of France, Francis. She had decided to have her daughter carried to France to be brought up at King Henri's court, however unsuitable the Valois surroundings were for a young girl. When Mary was six, the time to leave for France had come.

The year before, Villegagnon had been made an officer in the French Royal Navy, where he had the opportunity to make use of the training he had acquired in Malta. He was eventually given command of the fleet which was to convey troops to Scotland to help the Queen Regent, and bring back the little Queen Mary. It was a chivalrous undertaking: at any rate, many French noblemen saw it in that light and volunteered to go. They were under the command of the Comte d'Essé and among them were some whose names were among the greatest in France. One of them was François de Chatillon, Comte d'Andelot, Admiral de Coligny's brother. He and his two brothers seem to have been Marie de Guise's personal friends, and they were distant cousins.

The troops gathered in Brittany and were shipped to Scotland in the spring of 1548. They landed at Leith and Villegagnon and his companions went to pay homage to the Queen and the Regent at Edinburgh Castle. The little Queen's retinue was drawn up: she was to be escorted to France by her governess, the beautiful Lady Fleming, her four Maries and several noblemen, including Lord Erskine and Lord Livingstone. They went on board *La Reale*, Villegagnon's flagship, while his companions were given commands in the army.[1]

Villegagnon put to sea; the crossing was long and so rough that Lady Fleming, who could not stand the pitching and tossing, implored the admiral to put back to Scotland. Villegagnon flatly refused: they would go straight to France or sink. Lady Fleming had to submit.

They did not sink and eventually reached Roscoff in Brittany, where the French Court had gathered to greet the little Queen. She was received in great state and the Court moved back to Paris with the five young Scottish girls and their escort. As for Lady Fleming, she promptly became Henri II's mistress and bore him a son.

Villegagnon sailed back to Scotland. During his absence, one of the leaders of the Frenchmen was d'Andelot, who had the soundest and clearest head in the group, the one whose advice was always sought. War-like operations were carried out round Edinburgh, Leith, Jedburgh, Haddington and North Berwick. They were erratic and very complicated.[2] At one time, it was thought that d'Andelot had been killed but it was a false report and the young leader (he was twenty-four) continued to direct operations. By the beginning of 1549 they were more intricate than ever. The French troops were better equipped than the Scots. In March, Villegagnon sold a gun to the High Treasurer of Scotland for £32 6s.[3]

Yet everything—and even warfare in Scotland—comes to an end. Villegagnon was short of money and he wrote to the Guise princes, asking for a hundred *écus* each month.[4] He had received nothing for a long time and also asked for food and reinforcements. Both were badly needed. Villegagnon also asked to be protected against a man who was becoming troublesome, though not actually dangerous, in spite of a rather ominous past: he had killed a man in a Roman church. This was rather too daring a gesture to make people round him feel particularly comfortable.[5]

Eventually things calmed down. Villegagnon went to England to discuss the exchange of prisoners of war. Edward VI had given him a safe-conduct in which he was described as 'M. de Veale Gangeoun, Knight of St John and General in the service of the French King'.[6] He returned to Scotland when his mission had been carried out, collected his men and sailed back to France. Before they left, the Queen Regent came to visit them and made a pleasant little speech of thanks.

Back in France Villegagnon was appointed Vice-Admiral of Brittany and given the estates of Tournan and Torcy, not far from Paris. Yet he did not stay long on the Continent. Having been for almost a year in a very northern climate, he was possibly longing for Maltese heat and sunshine; so shortly afterwards he sailed back to the island, hoping to secure pro-motion. He brought news to Malta which was not exactly pleasant: he knew from reliable sources that the Turks were going to attack the island, as well as Tripoli, very soon. He did all he could to make the Grand Master d'Homedes realize what it meant and act accordingly. D'Homedes probably understood, but he refused to do anything, either to repair fortifications or to send adequate reinforcements to Tripoli. Was he a miser, a stubborn fool, a traitor or all of these? Whatever it was, Villegagnon failed to rouse him.

Gozo was looted by the Turks because it was undefended,

and its inhabitants sold into slavery. D'Homedes had actually refused to shelter women and children in Malta. Sick at heart, Villegagnon went to Tripoli as a volunteer, to fight under the Governor Jean de la Valette. The Turks came, led by Dragut. The small garrison fought to the end. They were heavily outnumbered by the invaders and had to sail away: Tripoli was hopeless from the start, but the Knights had not been given a fair chance.

Villegagnon was indignant. He left for France at once and published another letter, in which he flatly accused d'Homedes of having put into his own pocket the money which should have been spent on fortifying Gozo and Tripoli. When d'Homedes died, two years later, it was discovered that most of his fortune, instead of being bequeathed to the Order, as it should have been, went to his family in Spain. He was almost refused a State burial.

Back in France Villegagnon was sent to Brittany to fortify Brest, but he quarrelled with the Governor and left. Then something quite surprising happened: he became a Protestant. He may have been sincere of course. Judging by his writings during the next years, he was well informed concerning his new religion and its main issues, but in the light of later events it seems more likely that his conversion was merely formal. What he had said and written against d'Homedes and the Order had been so violent that a complete break was necessary. A change of religion provided him with the required dramatic gesture. As for his faith, it is likely that he never had any.

He soon made contact with Coligny. He may have been introduced to him by the latter's younger brother, d'Andelot, his friend in Scotland, who had been the first of the three brothers to become a Protestant. But Gaspard de Coligny was much more than the leader of a religious party: with forethought far ahead of his time, he was planning the conquest of overseas territories, so as to check the dangerous Spanish hold on South America. He was endeavouring to send Protestant emigrants to Brazil, and Villegagnon had heard of his scheme. He had not much to do at that time and he had cut himself off from Malta. He went to Coligny and the Admiral was attracted by Villegagnon's intelligence and enterprise. He may not have noticed the man's violent and restless temper, but he duly commissioned Villegagnon to lead a group of Protestants to colonize part of Brazil. Villegagnon was, or believed himself to be, sick of the Order and of Europe, seeking only an opportunity to leave the Old World for one where he could live in peace according to the Scriptures.

So he sailed in November 1555 with a small group, which eventually landed in Brazil, where they founded 'Antarctic France', the main settlement of which was named Fort Coligny. The usual troubles encountered by early colonies occurred in Brazil. Volunteers were few and badly prepared for their hard life. Some of them were most objectionable characters who merely wanted to get away from civilized surroundings. Villegagnon took no women: he may have thought it wise at first, but no colony could be permanently organized without them. There were hardly any stores. The settlers hoped to find a paradise, where life would be easy and carefree: they were badly shaken when they discovered what the New World was like.

Life there proved to be difficult and dangerous. Unexpected hardships harassed the colonists, yet Villegagnon at first succeeded in keeping some sort of order. Out of his three ships, he sent two back to Europe, with a request for more stores and reinforcements. By the same ship he sent a letter to Calvin, in Geneva, dated September 16, 1556; it was both affectionate and respectful. He related the story of his journey, gave a short and rather optimistic account of the state of the colony, asked for new settlers (with wives and children, this time) and, above all, for pastors to organize a church. Eventually, a small group of fourteen people decided to go; among them were two pastors, G. Chartier and P. Richer, together with a young man who was to become the historian of the colony, Jean de Léry. More joined them and eventually about eighty people left with M. de Bois le Comte, Villegagnon's nephew. On their way to Honfleur, whence they were to sail, they called on Coligny at his castle of Chatillon-sur-Loing, where they were entertained and feasted by the Admiral. It seems strange that he never suspected Villegagnon of double-dealing: he was too upright a man to suspect others.

The crossing was long and bad. When the party reached Brazil, they were badly disappointed by what they found and things went from bad to worse. Living conditions were more than primitive, tempers became frayed, and to make things even more awkward, religious dissension set in. Villegagnon had behaved at first like a sincerely devout Protestant, sometimes going as far as taking services himself. Some of the prayers he wrote or improvised have been preserved: they are very fine, well conceived and well written. Then trouble began. According to Jean de Léry, he disagreed violently with the two pastors about the doctrine of Communion. Everybody became heated about it, which was not unusual in the sixteenth century. The whole colony began opposing Villegagnon on various grounds: he dressed gorgeously, changing his clothes every day and keeping for his own use material which should have been used to trade with the natives. Villegagnon was a handsome man and possibly vain. He was ambitious, too, and tried to rule his colony like a dictator. His companions refused to submit and, among other things, they stopped taking Communion with him and held their own services at night. Eventually rebellion broke out in earnest. Villegagnon had three men executed. Most of his former companions left, dreading the same fate, Jean de Léry among them, and they had a terrible journey back to Europe.

Villegagnon was left without a coherent opposition and he became increasingly violent and cruel; then everything deteriorated quickly. The natives rebelled and in the end Villegagnon escaped secretly, sailing back to France and leaving his companions to fend for themselves. The end of the colony came shortly afterwards: the little group he had deserted was murdered by the natives and the Spaniards.

Villegagnon now changed sides once more and returned to Roman Catholicism. Catholic writers, like the historian Maimbourg in the seventeenth century, praised him for his 'return to the faith', which is rather over-optimistic. The only explanation of Villegagnon's repeated apostasies and shameful behaviour is rather the fact that he never believed in anything, Calvin had judged him clearly and had published the fact that the man was an atheist. Villegagnon pretended to be indignant and started a dispute with Calvin. In 1560, in a letter to the Genevese authorities, he attempted to justify his behaviour in Brazil and his first books.[7] By that time Francis II of France was dead, the Protestant party was gaining strength at Court and in the kingdom and it might be possible for Villegagnon to recover the Admiral's favour. At least, he may have hoped to. Nothing came out of it, for Coligny was not to be deceived twice, so that in 1561 Villegagnon published *De biblio Gallico* against Calvin's doctrine of sacraments. He wanted to have a sort of summit talk and a public discussion. Calvin was quite willing, as it was dangerous to allow Villegagnon to continue unchecked. But apparently nothing came of this: Calvin or Beza would have been far too dangerous opponents, even for the clever Villegagnon.

Villegagnon had been reconciled with the Order of Malta. D'Homedes and the next Grand Master had died; the newly-elected Grand Master, Jean de la Valette, wanted men who could fight, and was not over-concerned about their morals. The Turks were threatening Malta and they struck in 1565. Yet Villegagnon was neither among the Knights who went back to the island before the beginning of the siege, nor among the 300 French volunteers. It was certainly not because he might have dreaded to face his former colleagues: he was quite without shame, and the reason was probably his age. He was fifty-five years old, which was quite a lot in the sixteenth century. He remained in France and eventually was given the Commandery of Beauvais and made Ambassador of the Order.

Villegagnon died in Beauvais in 1571. His former friend, François d'Andelot, had died in Saintes—possibly poisoned— in 1568. The little Queen whom Villegagnon had brought to France had become Dauphine and then Queen, once more, of another kingdom, and finally a widow at twenty. She had led a strange, unhappy, tempestuous life and was now a prisoner in England and her own worse enemy.

In a private collection in Malta there is a good sixteenth-century portrait of d'Andelot, painted when he was about twenty-five. Could it have been brought there by Villegagnon, as a present from the man who had been his friend and whose faith he was to betray?

31

CHAPTER III

THE MARSHAL DE TOURVILLE
AND FAIR ANDRONICA

~❦~

6 HE was very tall and well-proportioned, fair, re-
served, always well-dressed and courteous, always
in love with some girl; and with all that he had a
silly expression and an equally silly way of speaking. Yet he
had all the honesty, honour and easy, refined courage one
could wish for; he was born for the sea and for war. He was
kind, gentle, modest in the extreme, always ready to shield his
subalterns' blunders and extol their exploits, so that, from the
cabin boy to the officer in command, he was respected, admired
and worshipped by everyone in the navy.' Such is the portrait
Saint-Simon drew of Marshal Anne Hilarion de Costantin de
Tourville, for some years a Knight of Malta. All his contemporaries were impressed by his manly beauty and refinement.
His first biographer, the Abbé de Magron, who wrote in the
middle of the eighteenth century, also drew a portrait of his
hero: 'His hair was so golden that it was almost dazzling; his
eyes were blue, and to the gentleness such eyes usually re-
flect was added a brightness at which one could not easily
stare.' Throughout de Tourville's life his looks impressed those
who met him, and yet in his naval career he was spared neither
setbacks nor tragedy.

He was born in Normandy in 1642. His family was of old
and very noble stock, connected with some of the best in the
kingdom, but there were six brothers and sisters; thus the
family was not rich, and for this reason it was found expedient
to make the youngest boy a Knight of Malta. He was about
four when he was admitted into the Order as a Knight of
Minority, a title bestowed on those who joined when they
were still under twenty. De Tourville was about seventeen
when he went to Malta to make his vows. His striking aspect

2. Commander Laparelli's battle with Algerian vessels, 1736

Grand Master de Rohan's galley

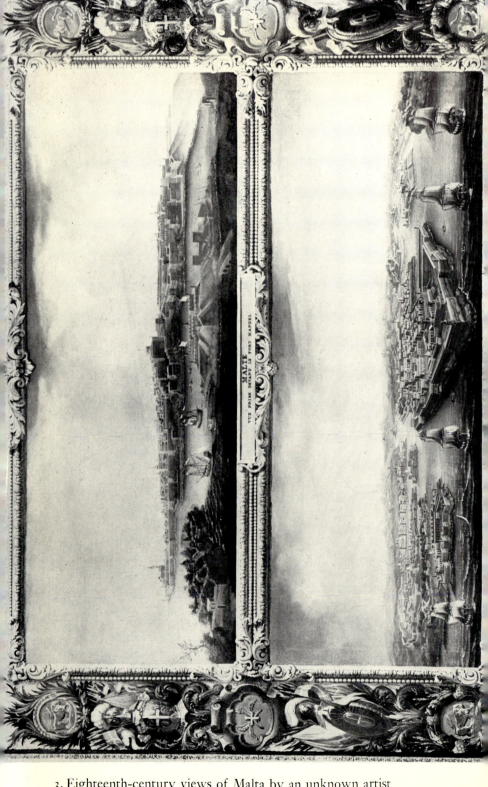

3. Eighteenth-century views of Malta by an unknown artist

was an asset and also a hindrance: handsome young men were often greeted with scathing remarks and unpleasant suggestions. Yet those who tried to make fun of de Tourville quickly discovered that the boy was not to be trifled with, for he could whip out his sword in a flash and use it with dangerous accuracy. He quickly fell in love with the sea and the ships, and proceeded to learn all about them. On December 29, 1661, he completed his second caravan and he was barely eighteen.[1] He sailed in the ship commanded by the Chevalier d'Hocquincourt, who was not much older than himself. At first d'Hocquincourt was not very pleased at having to take on board this striking-looking youth whose amateurishness he mistrusted; but his displeasure did not last long. De Tourville proved himself a born sailor: his cool courage delighted d'Hocquincourt, who soon became his friend, in spite of the younger man's undiminished passion for dressing himself beautifully and keeping spick and span in all circumstances. His colleagues often resented this characteristic and tried to make fun of it. He once challenged one of them to a race up the mast and down again and won, for he could do anything on board, despite his fine raiment.

He spent several seasons with d'Hocquincourt, fighting the Turks among the Greek islands which were the Order's happy hunting ground. The Greeks were not very well treated by the Knights, who sometimes looted the islands as a sort of training. They felt no obligation to be over-scrupulous towards schismatics. The Turks dreaded the Maltese galleys above everything, and the Knights were dangerous enemies. In 1661, d'Hocquincourt's vessel, together with one or two others, met a Turkish fleet near Coron. A short but violent fight ensued in which de Tourville played a leading part. He was wounded by a spear thrown at him by a Turk when the fight was almost ended. The wound looked dangerous and when the galley had entered the harbour of Syphanto to be repaired and to collect water and food, de Tourville was carried to the local doctor's house for more careful attention than he could expect on board.

What follows has been related by the Abbé de Magron, who wrote de Tourville's biography in 1758. It is quite possible, therefore, that the tale is fictitious, since the eighteenth century way of dealing with biography was not exactly reliable. Magron was also making use, nevertheless, of some perfectly accurate documents, and his story is amusing and full of colour.

The Syphanto doctor was a Signor Yani; he was a good doctor and a pleasant and refined man. He carefully probed and washed de Tourville's wounds and kept the young Knight in his house that he might attend him day and night. One of Yani's servants, a Moorish girl, had seen his patient from a distance and she gave a colourful description of him to Yani's daughter, Andronica. The girl was much interested and sent the servant to de Tourville with flowers and a charming message in Italian. De Tourville was still very weak and a little dazed, having lost much blood, yet he answered the letter, imploring its author to come and revive him with the sight of her beauty. The slave told him that Andronica was as chaste and witty as she was beautiful, and that he had no hope of seducing her. De Tourville replied that so horrible a thought could never enter his mind: was he not a Knight of Malta and had he not taken a vow of chastity?

In the doctor's house he was constantly visited by his friends, and d'Hocquincourt spent all his free time at his bedside. Now (and this is probably the proof that the whole story is heavily touched up) the slave was under the impression that her master's patient was a young woman of uncommon beauty, possibly the mistress of one of the Knights who often called at Yani's house. She imparted that piece of news to Andronica, who made no difficulty about visiting her father's guest. Andronica was most impressed by de Tourville's complexion and golden hair, and completely taken in by his soft, pleasant voice and charming manners. She also believed—or pretended to believe—that her father's patient was a young woman and she displayed the most touching and affectionate compassion. De Tourville was already feeling much better, and he returned the girl's affection, but confessed he was a man and had been wounded while fighting the Turks. He swore that he would treat her with the utmost respect, but he duly fell in love with her. She visited him daily, and when d'Hocquincourt called de Tourville could not refrain from telling him what had happened. D'Hocquincourt was greatly interested, and coming one day to see his friend, he found him completely recovered from his wound, kneeling at Andronica's feet and fondly kissing her hands.

By that time the ship had been repaired. De Tourville was well again and Malta was calling. The young man and the girl were in despair at the idea of parting, possibly for ever. De Tourville was madly in love and had no idea what to do. He decided, however, to take Andronica with him, vaguely thinking of leaving the Order to marry her. They decided where and when to meet. De Tourville arrived at the appointed place, waited for hours, but the girl never appeared. Finally, he left in despair. Later he received a letter from d'Hocquincourt, telling him that he had carried away the fair Andronica, who had been 'constantly faithful', though he did not say to whom. He treated the whole matter as a joke, and de Tourville thought it a bad one. He had lost his mistress, his friend and his ship, and was stranded and heartbroken. He eventually made his way back to Malta, called on the Grand Master Cottoner and gave him a carefully expurgated version of what had happened in Syphanto. Raphael Cottoner was broadminded and did not inquire too closely into what the young Knights—or the old ones—did, provided they fought well.

Shortly afterwards de Tourville heard of Yani's death. Before dying, the doctor had written to him, begging him to find Andronica, of whom he had heard nothing more. De Tourville went on fighting. After the leading part he had played in the battle of Coron, the Grand Master had put him in command of a small ship of the Order, his first command, and he continued to roam among the Greek islands, reaping glory, collecting valuable prizes and possibly still bewailing the loss of fair Andronica.

In 1662, during one of his cruises, he captured a Turkish ship and, while inspecting his prize, found several captives locked in a cabin. One of them was a young woman in the last stage of exhaustion and despair. Kind and courteous as usual, de Tourville knelt at her side and offered help and advice. She raised herself, revealing a beautiful, ashen face, and de Tourville recognized Andronica. She recognized him too and fainted in his arms. The young Knight, 'with a very sad countenance and full of grief', looked at the girl and knew he still loved her. There followed a long explanation, and no one knows just how passionate it was.

De Tourville's ship sailed for Venice, possibly for a thorough overhaul. He had Andronica with him and was again wondering what to do with the girl he loved, as he could not take her back to Malta. She suggested that she could go into a convent in Venice, a discreet, respectable shelter. De Tourville thought the idea an excellent one and probably offered to pay her keep. As soon as they landed he had to busy himself with his ship and attend to the numerous tasks and functions that befall a commanding officer. He was more than a mere sea captain: he was one of the leading Malta corsairs at an age when most of his contemporaries were just plodding their way through their first caravans.* The Doge received him and, like everyone else, was impressed by his youthful beauty. What with receptions, meetings, dockyard attendance and parties, de Tourville was frantically busy and had little time to devote to Andronica, though he certainly called often at her convent.

He had to leave Venice and sail his ship back to Malta, where he was ecstatically received, and there he again met d'Hocquincourt, from whom he had been estranged for some months. Revived by glory and triumph, de Tourville forgave his friend and even told him of the last episodes of Andronica's story, which surprised d'Hocquincourt very much, for he thought she was dead and had already forgotten her. Shortly afterwards, d'Hocquincourt fell seriously ill of a fever and de Tourville looked after him during his sickness, all bitterness forgotten. When he was well again, they both retired to their ship, reunited to roam the seas together. There were quieter intervals when the young Knights lived up to their glamorous reputation. They spent the carnival in Rome, and it was a riotous time, during which an intriguing veiled lady started a romantic literary flirtation with de Tourville, which led to even more romantic meetings. De Tourville was maturing quickly and could not pine for ever for Andronica in her Venetian convent.

In fact, she had left it and was no longer pining, if she ever

---

* A journey at sea, undertaken on one of the Order's ships, to fight the Turks and acquire naval training. Before taking their vows, Knights had to make three or four caravans.

did. When de Tourville returned to Venice in 1665, he went to the convent at once and was told by the Mother Superior that Andronica had left. She was now the wife of a senator. In true conformity to the best traditions of the *comedia dell' arte*, the senator was old and doted over his beautiful young wife. De Tourville and Andronica met again, and it was a most sentimental encounter. In accordance with what was expected of an old Venetian senator, he noticed or suspected nothing and was greatly flattered by the attention paid to his wife by the dashing young Knight of Malta. It was carnival time again—in Venice there were several carnivals a year— and life was gayer than ever. De Tourville went everywhere with d'Hocquincourt and another gay young fellow, the Chevalier de Bavière. There were several ladies with them, including Andronica and a beautiful girl who used to visit de Tourville dressed as a page.

But that was the end of a gay and hectic life. The next year d'Hocquincourt's ship ran aground on a Greek island, Karpathos, driven there by a terrible Mediterranean gale. The ship split on the rocks, 170 men were drowned, including d'Hocquincourt, who had done everything so save his men and his ship. De Tourville was one of the few survivors: he had vainly tried to save his friend.

When he reached Malta, sick at heart, his prospects were very dark indeed. With the ship he had lost not only a good friend, but all his worldly wealth, for all his money was invested in her. He grieved for d'Hocquincourt and was very ill: he was already suffering from tuberculosis, and the rest of his life was a protracted fight against sickness. It was a miracle that he lived to be sixty-four.

He returned to France, seeing no future. His youth was behind him, though he was barely twenty-six. Then a new career opened for him in the French Navy, and a brilliant, though not altogether happy, life. But he left the Order of Malta first, serving now only under the French flag, and was eventually released from his vows.

CHAPTER IV

A PROTESTANT KNIGHT
GABRIEL DE TÉMÉRICOURT

❧ ❦ ❧

D E TOURVILLE'S adventures among the Greek islands
give some idea of the varied activities of the Knights
of Malta in the second half of the seventeenth century.
But their real purpose was to fight the infidel wherever and
whenever he could be found, and the eastern Mediterranean
was the ground in which the hunt was most productive. The
Order's accumulated energies were engaged in merciless warfare, for the Turks were still very dangerous; their navy was
powerful and they were good sailors. But the Order's fleet was
also led by daring men, accustomed to taking great risks. What
such men did when not fighting was quite another matter: the
rules were very strict but were usually neglected, and men
who continually risked their freedom and their lives at sea
were not to be worried too much. The Grand Masters knew
when to avoid seeing things that were quite obvious to others.
Such an understanding of the Order's regulations accounts for
the bewildering story of Gabriel de Téméricourt.

TO THE MEMORY
OF MAXIMILIEN D'ABOS DE TÉMÉRICOURT
KNIGHT OF MALTA
SEPTEMBER 1645-JUNE 1669
WHO DIED FOR THE FAITH
FIGHTING AGAINST THE TURKS
AND TO THE MEMORY
OF GABRIEL DE TÉMÉRICOURT
KNIGHT OF MALTA
CALLED THE SCOURGE OF THE SEA
SEPTEMBER 15, 1646-NOVEMBER 1672
MARTYRED BY MAHOMET IV
AS HE REFUSED TO COMMIT APOSTASY

So runs the inscription on the monument erected in the little church of Téméricourt, in the Vexin, to the memory of the two brothers. The family hailed from Béarn and had settled in the Ile de France later. It had been Protestant for some time, but the brothers' grandfather had returned to the Roman faith. Gabriel and Maximilien were entered for the Order of Malta when very young and Gabriel was one of the Grand Master's pages for two years, when about twelve years old. He returned with his brother to make their caravans and take their vows, and it was soon obvious that both brothers, despite their youth, were to rank with the best fighters ever to wear the eight-pointed cross.

On August 5, 1663, shortly after he had arrived in Malta, Gabriel was allowed to sail as a corsair under the Order's flag: he was then barely seventeen.[1] Within a few months he was in command of his own ship and so was Maximilien. They were to display the most outstanding talent and prove themselves as quite exceptional among the sailors of the Order, which meant a great deal. The younger brother was possibly the tougher: he was a short, fair-haired, good-looking lad, with pleasant blue eyes in a long, finely-chiselled face. This mild aspect was quite misleading: Gabriel de Téméricourt could display the utmost fury and violence. He and his brother hunted the enemy together, with one or two friends who were also in command of their own ships, and he fully deserved the name given him by the Turks, 'the Scourge of the Sea'.

In 1665, together with the Chevalier d'Éscrainville, the brothers pounced on an Egyptian fleet off Samos and captured three vessels. Five years later, Gabriel and Maximilien on their frigates, together with the Chevalier de Verrüe and the Chevalier de Brémond on smaller vessels, were refitting at Nio, among the Greek islands. They were suddenly warned that a fleet of about fifty Turkish galleys had been sighted. This was Mustapha Kaplan bringing reinforcements to the Turks besieging Crete. The four young men immediately sailed towards the enemy, who was taken completely unaware. It was a furious four days' battle, at the end of which the ships from Malta were victorious. Both brothers had sustained light wounds. They were victorious again in 1669, but in the same year, during another sea fight, Maximilien was grievously wounded in the head. He realized that he had not long to live, but with dogged courage he remained on deck until the day was won and the Turkish ship was sinking in flames. Then he collapsed and two days later died.

Gabriel went on fighting, with even greater daring. A Knight who saw him in action described him as 'one of the greatest captains known for many years'. Twice, in 1671, he attacked Turkish squadrons. The second time he fought alone against five ships and defended himself with such fury that he was able to tear himself free.

It is obvious that a man who led such a dangerous life would not be bothered much with scruples. Fire ran in Téméricourt's blood. Once, when looting the island of Mykonos, he freed the slaves of a Greek interpreter named Panagotti. Apart from that highly respectable profession, Panagotti was a slave dealer, specializing in beautiful young women whom he trained for the Sultan's pleasure. One of his favourite slaves was a Polish girl of great beauty, with whom he professed to be in love. When Téméricourt came to Mykonos to refit, one of Panagotti's captives succeeded in acquainting him with the sad plight of her companions. Téméricourt and his men stormed the house and liberated the women, including the lovely Pole. Panagotti implored Téméricourt to let him keep his favourite slave at least, and offered a big price for the favour, but the girl threw herself at the young Knight's feet and begged him not to sell her back into slavery, adding that she was of very noble parentage. Téméricourt 'respected the young person's quality and merit' and flatly refused to grant the pimp's request. Panagotti swore to be revenged.[2]

The Chevalier d'Arvieux,[3] the French Consul in Smyrna, knew Téméricourt and hated him. He had tried to stop 'his usual disorderly conduct' in Milo, which he looted after his expedition to Mykonos. Téméricourt had seen him, had promised everything and had not kept his promise. The Greek islands and their inhabitants were protected more or less by the King of France, and his consul did not like such unruly behaviour. In 1671 a French fleet commanded by the Marquis de Preuilly d'Humières came to the archipelago. Preuilly also met the young corsair and soundly berated him. Gabriel de Téméricourt renewed his promises, but again did not keep them. He was a nightmare to high officials in the Greek islands.

The dauntless young man who had always triumphed over his enemies was to be defeated by the elements. On October 28, 1671, as he was escorting prize ships to Malta, he was caught in one of the terrible gales which sweep the Mediterranean in the autumn, and his ship ran aground on the coast of Tripoli. Téméricourt swam ashore but was taken prisoner, recognized and strictly watched. For some time he hoped that he might be ransomed by the Order. The Grand Master was not generous, but he himself was rich, after his glorious and profitable campaigns at sea.

However, the situation deteriorated very quickly. Téméricourt knew that a price had been put on his head and his enemies gloated over the capture of the 'Scourge of the Sea'. 'He was much too well recommended,' sneered d'Arvieux when telling the story in his memoirs. The young man was taken to Andrianople to meet the Sultan: he had not abandoned hope and, when questioned, begged for time and offered a big ransom. He might have succeeded even then, but for a stroke of extraordinarily bad luck: the interpreter was the notorious Panagotti, the Greek from Mykonos, who was still smarting over the loss of his Polish slave. Panagotti now extracted his revenge and induced the Sultan to refuse ransom, explaining that the man was a criminal who had robbed him of the beautiful slave he was keeping for the Sultan's seraglio. Yet the Sultan was impressed by Téméricourt's youth and lofty behaviour. He had never seen 'so much majesty in such a humiliating situation', wrote an eye-witness, quoted by Des Barres in his *Etat présent de l'Archipel*. Téméricourt was granted some respite. He had been such a magnificent leader at sea that the Sultan tried to win him over to the Moslem faith. The young man was taken to a tolerable prison and made as comfortable as possible. He was offered money, the rank of Admiral and even a princess of royal blood in marriage, provided he would renounce his faith and become a Moslem. In fact, they dangled before him 'all that might attract a young warrior'. It was of no avail and the Sultan changed his tactics, to Panagotti's delight. Téméricourt was sent to the common prison and to the stocks, among murderers and common robbers. Yet his servant Paul, a converted Turk, had not been taken from him and still ministered as much as he could to his master's needs. Témécourt never flinched.

In his prison he was visited by two men who could bear witness to his outstanding courage. One was a French adventurer, La Magdelaine, who, though the slave of a high Turkish dignitary, enjoyed great liberty and was eventually set free. The other was a German lord, whom des Barres met and interviewed; this German may have known the young man before his capture and it is a pity des Barres does not give his name.[4]

For a fortnight Témécourt was tortured 'in body and limb', but neither hunger, nor the scourge, nor the rack could conquer him. 'This captive body was possessed of a heart which had always scorned death, and he accepted it rather than death of his soul,' wrote La Magdelaine. Nothing could break his will, and in the end he was beheaded. The mutilated corpse remained on show outside the prison for a week and was then thrown into the river. It seems that Capuchin monks managed to steal the severed head and wrote an account of his death. Both the head and the account have disappeared. They possibly thought that the Order of St John might try to have this very genuine martyr beatified. D'Arvieux, who hated him, yet went so far as to write: 'So he atoned for his past misdeeds, and his constancy in his faith may bring people to look on him as a martyr.' Obviously, the man was moved in spite of himself.

One does indeed wonder why the Order did so little to publicize the heroic death of the young 'Scourge of the Sea'. The fact that he had led a riotous life in the Greek islands and possibly elsewhere was of no great importance, as the Greeks were schismatics and most Knights behaved in exactly the same way. No one seems to have wondered at that strange lack of gratitude from an Order the young man had served so well: yet it is both surprising and shocking. The reason may be that the Grand Master knew, or suspected, part of a rather surprising truth.

In 1671, Jean Chardin, a French jeweller, arrived in Smyrna on his way to Persia to sell precious stones to the Shah. He at once called on the French Consul, who was delighted to see an intelligent and cultured young countryman, and they chatted for a long time. The Consul complained of the innumerable problems which weighed upon him in Smyrna: life was difficult; among other things, the Greek seas were alive with pirates of all kinds and from places as varied as Majorca, Villefranche, Leghorn and Malta, and they were all equally repellent. The Consul went on: 'I cannot forget the answer one corsair, the Chevalier de Téméricourt, made . . . to the Marquis de Preuilly, who was on one of the King's ships, the *Diamant*. They met in Milo and the Chevalier was the guest of the Marquis. As they happened to be talking about corsairs, he asked the latter: "Now, Chevalier, tell me, all these rapes, slaughters, sacrileges you commit every day, your blasphemies and in short all your barbarous godless deeds, don't they make you dread some sort of retribution? Don't you believe in Hell?" "Indeed not!" replied the Chevalier. "I am a Lutheran. I don't believe in any of those things." Such was the corsairs' attitude!'[5]

It is perfectly true that Preuilly d'Humières was in the Greek islands in that time, after leading ships to Crete, and also that he met Téméricourt: Arvieux also describes their stormy meeting, but he does not give the young man's surprising retort. One might assume at first glance that Téméricourt gave the first answer that might floor a too insistent senior officer who was getting on his nerves.

Yet this was not so. Chardin, when reporting this incident, knew precisely what he was talking about. He himself was a Protestant, and a few years later, on his return from Persia, discovered that he had no future in France because of his religion, and therefore emigrated to England, where he was warmly welcomed by Charles II, knighted and given diplomatic employment. Thus he understood Téméricourt's position well: the young man's answer was a definite statement of fact, and not merely a way to rid himself of a bore. Less than two years later he was to endure imprisonment, torture and death for his faith. There is no reason to think that he lied to Preuilly when the whole thing was of no importance whatever. He may have led a riotous life: it meant nothing against the seriousness of his deeper belief. The wording of his statement was of course crude: the Lutheran doctrine certainly accepts the dogmas of Paradise and Hell, but what he possibly meant was that he accepted the notion that man can do nothing for his own salvation, which depend's on God's grace alone. Had Preuilly been a subtler theologian—if a theologian at all—he might have continued the discussion, but he knew even less than his youthful opponent, and he was taken aback by the rejoinder.

There are one or two further details worth noticing. On the monument in the village church it is stated that Gabriel died a martyr 'as he refused to commit apostasy' (in French: *refusant d'apostasier*), while his brother is mentioned as having 'died for the Faith'. The difference probably comes from the fact that the brothers' faiths were not identical, and that Gabriel's faith was not *the* one faith according to Roman Catholic notions, and anyone, even a Protestant, who refuses to become a Moslem 'refuses to commit apostasy'. One observes that in describing the young man's captivity and death La Magdelaine speaks of his bravery and steadiness, but says nothing about any regret at not being attended by a priest to absolve him after a fairly eventful life: he needed nothing of the sort and accepted no intermediary between God and himself.

It is likely that Nicolas Cottoner, the Grand Master, knew this fantastic story: Gabriel de Tém300ricourt seems to have been perfectly candid about it. Cottoner must have been a broad-minded man, and we shall see further instances of his pleasant turn of mind. Much was forgiven this impetuous young man who was such a superb officer. As for Téméricourt, he probably never hesitated about serving under the eight-pointed cross: he loved adventure, danger, the sea and all the excitement of his chosen career. Besides, in 1671, because of his religion he could not have served in the French Navy: at that time Louis XIV was hounding Protestants out of all places and offices, including the fighting services.

One more point has to be explained: how was it that Téméricourt was a Lutheran, while almost all French Protestants are and were Calvinists? The few Lutherans in France originated in the eastern parts with which Téméricourt had no connection. Chardin himself was a Calvinist and in using the word 'Lutheran' could not have done so without consideration.

There are various possible explanations of this point. For instance, it seems likely that Téméricourt had been converted in Malta: neither Maximilien, nor his brothers and sisters in France, were Protestant, but the Swedish volunteers in Valetta were all Lutherans, and one of them may have been responsible for Téméricourt's conversion.

In 1644, the Langue* d'Allemagne in Valetta went out of its way to accept 'with pleasure' a Swedish Knight, Jean-Robert de Staël, a member of an Esthonian family who had assumed Swedish nationality earlier in the century and was shortly to revive the old family name of Staël-Holstein.[6] As he joined the Order of Malta as a Knight of Justice, duly entered into one of the Langues, it was reasonable to believe that he became a Roman Catholic. But he did not. In August 1678 a Commander of Schmissing wrote in French to an English diplomat:

'Sir. As I have always retained a vivid remembrance of Your Excellency's gracious attitude towards me when I had the honour to meet him at the Cologne conference, I trust in your generosity and kindness to receive my humble duties; at the same time, may I beg for your powerful support, to recommend to His Britannic Majesty the Chevalier Jean-Robert de Staël, who, while on his way to Malta to serve our Order a few months ago, was taken prisoner by a corsair's ship and conveyed to Algiers, where he is now a slave in chains. And as the Infidels always believe that a Knight of Malta can pay a large ransom, there is very little hope that this unhappy gentleman will ever be rescued from his present plight.'

His family was poor and his only hope was to be redeemed by Charles II.[7] Grand Master Cottoner also wrote to the King on the captive's behalf, to ask that Sir John Narbrough, who was about to sail for Algiers, should be instructed to ransom de Staël. Apparently de Staël was brought back, for he was a captain in the Swedish army in 1682 and died in Sweden in 1694.

The only explanation as to why the Grand Master and de Staël's friend had applied to the King of England for assistance

* The Order had formerly been divided into eight *Langues,* more or less according to the allegiance of their members; France, Provence, Auvergne, England, Italy, Germany, Aragon, Castille and Portugal (joined). England seceded at the Reformation.

is that he was the sovereign who undertook to redeem Protestant captives, while Louis XIV did the same for Roman Catholics. De Staël, though a professing Knight of St John and member of the Langue d'Allemagne, had undoubtedly remained a Protestant. He was probably a staunch one, for to join the Order without renouncing his faith would have caused him much trouble. Putting his trust in Charles II may have been risky: Charles was kind and compassionate, while his cousin of France was not, but terribly short of money. However, de Staël was lucky.

There is no proof that he was the man who converted Téméricourt: he was not the only Swede in Malta. Yet, a man who had taken so much trouble and ran so many risks to remain true to his religion may have been daring and patient enough to awaken a flicker of religious faith in the soul of a tough and passionate young man.

CHAPTER V

THE COLOURFUL LIFE OF
KARL JOHANN VON KÖNIGSMARK

⭐❀⭐

IN the last chapter mention was made of the fact that young Swedish noblemen often served as volunteers with the Order's crews. A few years in the Mediterranean gave them a sound naval training in totally new surroundings. Some of the greatest Swedish names are found among them. They were welcomed by their companions, who bore no ill-will towards Scandinavians, despite the fact that the commanderies of the Priory of Dacia had been confiscated by Sweden and Denmark when both countries went over to the reformed Church. The Order had raised a mild protest and, as nothing developed, had accepted the situation with equanimity. They knew exactly when it would be unseemly to drive a protest too far. They also knew that it would have been of no avail.

In 1677 Count Karl Johann von Königsmark arrived in Malta to serve in the navy. He was eighteen, with handsome, refined features, large bold blue eyes, and a mass of curly golden hair which enabled him to dispense with a wig. He was not very tall, but he was both tough and graceful. This pleasant young man was the scion of an outstandingly unconventional family. His father had been a companion of Gustavus Adolphus during the Thirty Years' War. One of his uncles commanded a regiment in the French service: he was one of those captain-adventurers who followed their own whims across Europe, looking for employment and adventure, and welcoming both. Karl Johann had two sisters and a younger brother. One of the sisters was to live an uneventful life in Sweden, but the other, the beautiful Maria-Aurora, was to become the Elector of Saxony's mistress, and their son, Count Maurice of Saxony, was to serve France and become Marshal de Saxe, one of the best commanding officers in history. The brother, Philip

Christopher, was murdered in Hanover on the orders of the Elector and his mistress, for he was suspected of being the Electress Sophia-Dorothea's lover. All the Königsmarks were good-looking, intelligent and dauntless, and Karl Johann was possibly the hardiest of the family.

He was about sixteen when he left Sweden to try his luck abroad. First he went to France, where his uncle, Otto Wilhelm, commanded a regiment. The uncle was delighted by his tough and handsome nephew, and he accepted him as his boon companion, which was not the best possible training for a lad of that age. Königsmark proved himself to be above his reputation as, feeling bored with too tame a life, he decided to leave France and go to Malta as a volunteer in the hope of finding a more strenuous form of service at sea. It agreed with him, and he was revealed as a magnificent fighter with a fiery temper, and also a great success with the ladies. He was also very popular with his fellow Knights, who liked unconventional men. When Königsmark arrived in Malta, the war in Crete was over and had ended in defeat. The losses had been heavy and the Order wanted to reassert its presence in the eastern reaches of the Mediterranean. With that end in view it had to deal heavy blows at the Turks and reorganize its navy.

Königsmark's exploits were numerous. He loved his dangerous life at sea as much as his relaxation in Valetta when the ships returned to refit. One day the look-out of the galley in which he was serving saw in the distance two becalmed ships trying furiously to find some wind. They had a strange appearance and at closer quarters the Knights realized that one was a Christian ship which had been captured by pirates on the coast of Barbary; they were trying to make Tangier. The wind had fallen and they were motionless, the captor being obliged to stay by its prey. The Maltese galley rowed at top speed towards the enemy in order to board it. When the long-pointed prow of the galley crashed into the side of the Turkish ship, Königsmark was one of the first to grasp a rope and swing himself aboard. One of the Turks saw him just before he landed and cut the rope. In full armour the young man fell into the sea and sank, but he rose to the surface, swam back to the ship and somehow succeeded in hauling himself up. He reached the upper deck as pandemonium broke out,

4. Capture of a vessel by Maltese galleys under Commander de Boisbaudrant, 1644

Commander Laparelli's vessels in a fight with Algerians, November 5, 1736

The Right Hon:ble Charles John, Lord Konigsmarke,
Earle of Magdalene, & Wittemwocke, Lord of Rotenburg, & Ponhaven, &c.
Who was forced to acquaint from being an Accessory to ye barbarous murder of Mr Tho: Thÿnn Esq: &c Fatall's.

That thy Valour or to make thy Cause
The argent make that arrogance the cause,
And life this may require so terse in me,
And have harm's a penie no armall quite.

This will known Courage seeks as we demand,
Bethold than with a necessary hand,
So that who murther, who can dare by sight.

ANNE hILARION DE COTTENTIN COMTE DE TOVRVILLE
MARECHAL ET VICE AMIRAL DE FRANCE.

for the Turks had been overwhelmed by the Knights, who were fighting with deadly fury. Königsmark, who had kept his sword when falling, flung himself into the fray. At last the Turkish captain, seeing that there was no hope of freeing himself from the Maltese vessel, set fire to the magazine: the ship blew up and, with many others, Königsmark was hurled back into the water. This time he was wounded. Nevertheless, he succeeded in swimming back to his own ship and his companions helped him aboard, deeply impressed by his dogged courage. His wounds were attended to and, quite worn out by the violent action, he was able to snatch some sleep after he had been cheered by the staff and the crew of the galley.

On reaching Valetta he was carried in triumph to the Grand Master. Nicolas Cottoner had been a good naval officer in his youth and he was able to appreciate Königsmark's exploit to the full. To prove his gratitude and admiration he made him a Knight of Grace of St John of Jerusalem, though a Protestant.

A few months later, having recovered from his wounds, Karl Johann von Königsmark left Malta to find more excitement in other surroundings. His next port of call was Venice, and the next episode was equally romantic. He fell in love with a Countess of Southampton, who returned his infatuation. She was a small, plump woman with thick, dark, curly hair, a beautiful complexion, a small mouth and lovely teeth. She renounced her family and country and, dressed as his page, accompanied her lover everywhere. It does not mean that Karl Johann was faithful to her, but she was under his spell.[1]

The lovers did not stay long in Venice and they left for Spain. Königsmark there fell in love with a beautiful Spanish girl, and did what was expected of a really passionate lover: he fought bulls in her honour. In those days dogs were sent into the ring to worry the bull and to tire it a little, then amateur matadors stepped in and fought. 'Young Count Königsmark wanted to fight a bull for the girl he loved, who happened to be a friend of mine,' wrote Mme d'Aulnoy, who was visiting Spain at that time and seems to have been a genuine eye-witness. Bull fights lasted for several days and twenty bulls were sent out on the first day. Königsmark rode into the ring gorgeously attired and began worrying the bull, which charged his horse and wounded it in the leg. The horse fell, but Königsmark had managed to dismount and started to fight the bull on foot. He was wounded almost at once, but though he was bleeding profusely, he attacked the bull again, leaning on his valet's shoulder. He wanted to finish the brute off as quickly as possible, but he could only wound it again in the neck, unable to give it a death thrust. Then he turned to his lady; he kissed his sword while he gazed at her intently, collapsed in a dead faint, and was carried off, half dead, by his servants.

What became of the girl has not been recorded by Mme d'Aulnoy. Königsmark recovered and went back to Sweden at the end of several eventful years. By that time the Countess of Southampton, who had borne him a child, had retired to a convent, living there without taking the veil. But life in his native country was much too tame for this fiery youth, and in 1681 he sallied forth again, this time taking his younger brother, Philip Christopher, with him. The boy was fifteen, but an adventurous life never begins too early for a Königsmark. Both brothers were fated to die very young, after short lives crammed with adventure.

Their first port of call was London, where the younger brother was sent to Foubert's Academy, the fashionable finishing school for boys of good family. Karl Johann had not much to do and he led the gay, frivolous life of young noblemen at Charles II's court. Again he fell in love, this time with a beautiful girl of fourteen, Lady Elizabeth Ogle, nicknamed Countess Carrot on account of her flaming red hair. Though she was hardly more than a child, she was the widow of Henry Cavendish, Earl Ogle, who had died almost immediately after their marriage. Königsmark asked for the girl's hand from her guardian, a stern grandmother who turned down his proposal, possibly because the young man had very little money while Lady Elizabeth was an heiress.

Königsmark was both sad and indignant. He needed a change and went to Tangier as a volunteer in the small English expeditionary force. As usual he fought well and hard, under desperate conditions. When he returned he heard with disgust that the girl he still loved had been compelled to marry Thomas Thynne, a coarse Wiltshire squire whose huge fortune had made a big impression on Elizabeth's grandmother.

But apparently the girl was not lacking in character: she had allowed herself to be married to a man old enough to be her father, but had fled to Holland almost at once. There was also a rumour that the marriage was not valid.

Thynne was one of Monmouth's most determined partisans. The King hated him and so did many others. When Königsmark heard of the girl's marriage, he swore that he would be revenged and so he was. Thynne was found murdered in Pall Mall in January 1682. There were all sorts of wild rumours and Königsmark's name was mentioned at once. A Pole or Swede, Captain Wratz, was arrested as the author of the crime. He was Königsmark's friend and companion: they had been together in Africa, and Wratz was known as a brave and desperate character. Königsmark tried to flee the country and a price was put on his head. He was described as 'about 25 or 26, of low stature, fairly full set; fair, long hair, and a round face with a few pock-holes in it'. He was eventually arrested and brought back to London. Foubert, the head of the academy where the younger brother was studying, tried to influence the judge who was to try the case, Sir John Reresby. The King had the young man brought to Whitehall and questioned him in an obviously friendly way. It was even rumoured that Charles II, who hated Thynne, had known something of the plot and may have approved it. The only man who never confessed to anything was Karl Johann. During the trial his attitude was perfect; he was quiet, straightforward and dignified. The jury, half English and half Swedish, according to a foreigner's privileges, acquitted him, while the other men were found guilty and sentenced to death. Even very conformist, law-abiding people like Sir John Reresby and John Evelyn admired Wratz's cool courage and dignity when he went to his execution, though at the same time they were horrified at his complete lack of religion.

Königsmark left England at once with his brother. It is impossible to know whether he had been shaken by this unpleasant episode and whether he had been hurt by Elizabeth's indifference to his fate. In fact, the girl had completely forgotten him. A few months later she married Charles Seymour, Duke of Somerset.

Königsmark went to France and was received at Versailles.

He may have had an introduction from Charles II to the King of France, who took him into his service and made him a colonel of the Furstenberg regiment, a German regiment in the pay of France. He was actually on the threshold of a magnificent career, and within the next few years fought with his troops in Flanders and in Spain, being wounded in Cambrai. At court he was very popular among the younger members of the royal family, and when the Dauphin and the Duke of Bourbon rode in a large carrousel in June 1685, Königsmark was one of the performers. The theme was an episode in the conquest of Granada and the young man was one of the Abencerage knights, dressed in a glittering and exotic costume, with the motto *Deside entonces* on his shield.

But now he destroyed his career by his surprising fidelity to a religious ideal. He had always remained a Protestant, even when serving Venice or Malta. In October 1685, Louis XIV revoked the Edict of Nantes, which for about eighty years had guaranteed a certain freedom to French Protestants. The King personally requested Königsmark to change his religion, dangling before him the prospect of a high rank in the army and at Court. He expected instant compliance, as Königsmark had never been noted for austere living. The King was probably staggered by the answer he received. With the utmost respect, the young man replied: 'Sire, if I committed such treason towards God and my ancestors, I should be unworthy to serve you.' He resigned at once and left France.

Seventeenth-century characters are not easy to probe. Letters are not numerous and contemporary accounts do not shed much light on their most inward thoughts and feelings. Yet it is difficult not to sense a longing for death in Königsmark's closing years. When he left France he seems to have been at his wits' end. Of course, a man of his calibre could always find employment and he did, but it was a return more or less to a well-beaten track. His uncle, Otto Wilhelm, was still fighting for Venice against the Turks, so Karl Johann went to Venice too, and then pushed southwards to the Morea, where fighting had been going on for a long time. As usual, he displayed the utmost bravery. He led the attacking troops at Navarino and again at Argirocastro. Shortly afterwards he caught cold, went on fighting and led the assault against Negreponte; but by that time he was completely exhausted. He lingered for a few days and died of pleurisy and exhaustion in that town. He was barely twenty-seven and his death was mourned by the army, which had fallen under the spell of his reckless courage. Most of the authors of memoirs of the time, like the Marquis de Sourches and Saint-Simon, mention his death as being a great loss to the Christian army.

CHAPTER VI

A HOLY MAN IN MALTA
COMMANDER DUBOIS DE LA FERTÉ

⟿⟐⟐⟜

WHEN searching the records of seventeenth or eighteenth century Knights of Malta, a large number of hardy adventurers, great sailors or soldiers, cunning diplomats and many unpredictable characters who led original, unorthodox lives are to be found. There were heroes and martyrs among them, but very few saints. Yet there was at least one Knight who, with great modesty, lived a saintly life without any display of arrogance or complacency. His name was Gabriel Dubois de la Ferté, Commander of Thiéval.

There is an engraved portrait which gives some idea of his features.[1] They were not handsome. He wears a long wig and is dressed in the surcoat of the Order, the red *soubreveste* with the white cross, which was worn when fighting, and he holds a naked dagger. In spite of such military display, the man looks kind, refined and rather wistful. Under his portrait are engraved four doggerel lines:

> De la croix du Seigneur, je tire ma noblesse;
> Je fus le religieux, l'enfant et le soldat;
> J'en fis tous mes plaisirs et toute ma richesse;
> Par elle je vainquis le Grand Turc au combat.*

Gabriel de la Ferté would have loathed those mawkish lines, but his brothers had commissioned a local priest to write his biography and the portrait was probably engraved at the same time. They combine to enable a modern reader to understand the life and mind of a man who in Malta was quite exceptional.

---

*I draw my nobility from the Lord's Cross; I was a religious in orders, a child and a soldier for Him; the Cross was all my joy and treasure; through it I conquered the Sultan in the field.

He came of an ancient, noble, impecunious Anjou family: the sort of family who, generation after generation, used to send their younger sons to Malta. It was the only possible solution for Antoine Dubois de la Ferté and his wife, Marie des Forges, who had sixteen children. According to the eighteenth-century biographer, those children had delightful temperaments and were full of charity and kindness. Gabriel was born in 1644. Two brothers, at least, were chosen by their father to go to Malta and Gabriel was the younger. He had been a very good little boy. As he was afflicted with a bad stammer, his parents thought it was quite unnecessary to waste money on his studies, and he was just taught how to read and write. In spite of such inadequate schooling, he developed a gift for writing charming letters, some of which have been published by his biographer. His tutor was impressed by the child's moral refinement: he was 'as chaste as an angel' and as generous as his scanty financial means allowed. He had charming manners and never quarrelled with anybody, not even his brothers and sisters.

When he was fifteen he was received into the Order of Malta, and a few months later was sent to Valetta; but the Grand Master, Raphael Cottoner, had just issued a decree by which Knights could not take their vows until they were twenty-one. Consequently, la Ferté remained on the island for a few weeks only and then went home, having promised to come back four years later to assume the eight-pointed cross for good. Meanwhile, he joined the French Army as a *Gendarme de la Maison du Roi* and fought in three campaigns under Soubise. He also tried to catch up with his studies. He was still a model young man, averse to gambling and very careful about the morals of the other young men he associated with. Yet it seems that he avoided looking like a prig, for he had a number of devoted friends, and seventeenth-century young officers would not have borne a sanctimonius bore gladly.

When the time came for him to sail back to Malta, changes had occurred in his family. His eldest brother had died and the other Knight of Malta had secured release from his vows so that he might marry and assume his duties as his father's heir. There were several other brothers and Gabriel had no wish to abandon the Order. He sailed for Malta when he was twenty-four, and had a quick but very rough crossing. For two or three days the ship pitched and tossed across the Mediterranean and Gabriel learnt all about sea-sickness, of which he remained a victim for the whole of his seafaring career. He reached Valetta, more dead than alive, at the height of the Carnival, but this austere young man was more shocked than delighted by the riotous gaiety he witnessed. He found a much more congenial occupation: the war in Crete was at its height, and as the Grand Master was asking for volunteers, Gabriel de la Ferté, though he had not yet taken his vows, got himself accepted for service in Candia. He spent most of his small wealth buying his equipment. At the last minute, his brothers sent him a small sum of money which was heartily welcomed: it paid for his red surcoat with the white cross.

In spite of the constant help that was sent to Crete, the island had to be evacuated: the Turks were too powerful and too well organized, and there were too many rivalries between the Christian leaders. When the troops left the island, Gabriel de la Ferté sailed to France and served again in the French Army, fighting at Senef under Condé's orders. Apparently, in spite of pious protests made by his biographer, he was not too keen about joining the Order too young. When he finally took his vows, he knew and fully understood what he was doing. He had been keenly interested in his work at the Hospital, but a professing knight had other and more strenuous tasks to fulfil. As soon as he had taken his vows, he was appointed to the staff of one of the galleys.

Such employment proved unpleasant. He hated the sea and the sea hated him. Galleys were swift vessels; they lay low on the water and were violently rocked by waves and wind. Accommodation was primitive, to say the least. Novices were not allowed to take off their boots at night, so that they might be ready to get up at a moment's notice. They slept on benches without sheets, wrapped in their cloaks. Gabriel de la Ferté had passed that stage because he was a professing knight, but life on board was rough even for the staff of a galley. Meals were served on silver dishes, since the Order owned tons of silver and to use plate turned out to be more economical than using cheap crockery; but the food was only what could be expected on a small, overcrowded and overloaded ship. De la Ferté wrote to one of his brothers:

'We are running the great risk of doing simply nothing and growing bored stiff. I pray God He gives me plenty of patience, so that I can seize any opportunity which comes to me. It is no small sacrifice not to be permitted ashore, to feel the greatest disgust for the sea, to live in cramped quarters in stinking air, to sleep two by two on a table and never to be alone; but one must make good use of such unpleasantness to work out one's salvation.'

His galley did not remain as idle as he feared. It was sent to Negreponte, in the Morea, which was besieged by Venetian troops helped by a detachment sent by the Order.[2] The Knights failed to capture the city, which was held by a strong Turkish garrison. They were there at the height of summer, and the heat, added to everything else, made their plight very difficult indeed. All the Knights were ill and several died. La Ferté survived, though he too had been very ill and had not spared himself either when fighting or when looking after the sick and wounded. It required all his strength to go on: 'I am bored by this very strenuous life,' he wrote to his brother. 'It is very difficult to continue this campaign without falling sick from the poisonous air of this wretched country. But one is comforted when one thinks one is serving God.'

While in the Morea he rescued two Turkish girls. One he found pinned down in her gutted house. She had been wailing for help for three days and no one paid any attention. La Ferté was able to release her and he nursed her back to health. He took her to Malta and paid for her keep in a convent. The other was a girl of good family who had been captured and sold to a Maltese pirate. Realizing only too well what would be her fate, La Ferté went to see her and offered to ransom her if she agreed to become a Christian. The girl had no choice, of course, and accepted his offer. He put her into a nunnery too, where she worked at embroidery. It seems that in Malta, La Ferté was terrified of breaking his vow of chastity, possibly because he was simultaneously at the mercy of a strong conscience and a fiery temper, knowing well what temptation was though he struggled hard against it.

Gradually he became used to the Maltese climate, and he suffered less when he was at sea, though he was never free from sea-sickness and always hated the seafaring life. He decided to remain in Malta and not return to his native country until he had achieved what he probably did not dare to call his ambition, but what was the aim of every Knight in the Order: a commandery. His biographer sees in his decision the proof of a Christian ideal; but to be on the spot when a commandery fell vacant might also have been the best tactic. La Ferté made up his mind never to ask for, and never to refuse, anything which came his way, and when the Grand Master made him the captain of a galley, he accepted the rank at once, though he was still suffering from the aftermath of the Negreponte campaign. He had hoped to achieve his dearest wish of being promoted to the rank of commander without having to go back to sea, but he had still a long time to wait.

It was a hard and expensive life. The captain of a galley had to equip his ship at his own expense, refunding himself from the profits from the capture of enemy vessels. By that time, Dubois de la Ferté had been given various pensions and grants, but these were not enough and his family helped him to some extent. He wrote to his brother: 'You are quite right to blame me for having undertaken another cruise, as I am really not strong enough. I do so in spite of myself, but I have got to obey, as the Grand Master knew my good will and suggested I should do it. The mere wish of my superior is an order.' The Grand Master was only too glad to find a man who took his vow of obedience so seriously; such men were not very numerous in Malta.

Two successive Grand Masters had died, Cottoner and then Caraffa. In 1690 Adrien de Wignacourt was elected and he realized that nothing but empty promises and unpleasant employment had been lavished on La Ferté, who had not even dared to complain. Wignacourt undertook to put things right and he made La Ferté a Captain of the Casal (one of the six officers of high rank who supervised the defence of Valetta), and afterwards Procuror (treasurer) of the Order and next Supervisor of the galleys and the hospitals and a member of the Council of the Auberge de France. La Ferté was conscientious and reliable in the extreme, and his gifts were acknowledged at last. There were a few privileges attaching to his various jobs: his horse was looked after by the Grand Master's grooms and he had been offered residence in the Grand Master's palace, but he preferred to stay at the Auberge de France when he was in town, which was fairly often on account of his work at the hospital.

He had bought himself a house outside Valetta and he described his life in a letter to his brother. His easy, familiar style is quite delightful:

'I have taken a house where I am extremely comfortable. I have a very pretty garden full of trees. I look after them, and the fruit they yield each year reproach me secretly for being the barren tree of the Gospel, which is just fit to be thrown into the fire. I have more than thirty pairs of doves of various kinds, some of which are not known in France. I often talk to them. Their whiteness and their gentleness teach me purity and innocence, their flight is a pretty lesson of how to soar to God, and as they have no malice they encourage me to bear no malice towards anybody.'

One of his neighbours once stole some of his birds. Dubois de la Ferté learned who was the thief, went to his house and said: 'Here is some money: buy yourself some doves if you need them, but please leave mine alone!'

Five or six of his friends, former Captains of the Galleys like himself, had formed a small religious community, living together in a single house, praying and tending the sick. 'They have resolved to make a saint of me,' la Ferté wrote to his brother, and he often visited them and stayed with them for several days; but he had too many commitments to allow him to lead a purely contemplative life, and it would not have agreed with his extremely active personality. According to him, Knights of Malta were now leading much more respectable lives than a few years earlier: it may not have been true, or there may have been a good number of Knights who led different lives, but if there was anyone to set a good example it was certainly this charming and modest man.

Yet the commandery he longed for was not forthcoming. Few commanders died, and in spite of his devoutness he bitterly complained to his brother of the endless and perhaps hopeless waiting. He was now fifty-one and his prospects were as vague as ever. Suddenly, one of the commanders did die (du Planty-Landereau) and the Grand Master gave his estate to la Ferté immediately. The estate was that of Thiéval, near Laval on the Maine, not very far from the Ferté family's estates. Planty-Landereau died in November 1695, and by the beginning of December la Ferté had left Malta for ever.

His last crossing was terrible: the Mediterranean is never friendly in winter and this time it surpassed itself. When la Ferté reached his brother's chateau on Christmas Eve he looked like a ghost, and his brother, who had not seen him for eighteen years, did not recognize him. He and his wife made la Ferté stay with them until he had completely recovered and for several months he lived in their chateau, dividing his time between his religious duties and his family. He could not avoid a minimum of social intercourse with his brother's neighbours, and yet he tried to lead an almost monastic life, looking after poor people, nursing the sick and practising an active, intelligent kind of charity, much assisted by his sister-in-law, who had quite fallen under his spell. But his young nephew's tutor, though a priest, said that the Commander went too far, and that he was disgusted, to the point of being literally sick, when he had to follow la Ferté to the bedside of an old man dying of dropsy.

When the commandery had been properly repaired and the Commander had been nursed back to health, he went to live at Thiéval and was promptly adored by all the poor of the neighbourhood. From his naval career he had retained the habit of (and possibly the taste for) doing any kind of job and mending anything, and in his pockets he always carried a hammer and pincers to mend and fasten sick people's windows. One day he met a beggar in rags and gave him his shirt. His biographer gives a detailed account of how he did so, as a seventeenth-century gentleman could not undress as easily and publicly as St Martin of old: 'Drawing aside,' he writes, 'the Commander pulled his fustian vest or shirt from under his coat and gave it him.' La Ferté's life is full of similar episodes, while he managed nevertheless to maintain his social rank, to accept invitations from his neighbours, and to reciprocate by sending presents of game and fruit, since his household was too primitive to allow him to entertain.

On the whole he was badly served, for he took some of the people he cared for as his valets, gave them little to do, was mostly concerned with moral welfare, and spent his time preventing them from swearing and cursing. He paid them very regularly, which was quite unusual at that time. He spent most of his income from the commandery on charity, fed badly, and wore himself out in his constant attempts to relieve the destitute. One of his chief cares, both in Anjou and in Malta, was coming to the rescue of fallen women and trying to bring them back to a better way of life.

La Ferté's life grew more and more austere, though he seems to have managed not to worry his relatives and friends by displaying the hardships he inflicted on himself. During the very severe winter of 1702 he caught a cold, did not look after himself properly, and the unattended cold developed into bronchitis and pneumonia. After a few days he passed peacefully away and was buried in the little chapel of his commandery: he was sixty.

Ten years later, at the request of his brothers, a local priest wrote his biography. The little book is very edifying and quite charming. The author, Joseph Grandet, had had access to many family documents and the Commander's letters, and he used them well. It may have been an attempt to secure the Commander's beatification, as his exemplary piety and saintliness were heavily stressed. However, the attempt did not get far. So much the better: this modest, pleasant man might have resented too great a posthumous glory.

CHAPTER VII

THE MAN WHO WOULD NOT DIE
COMMANDER DE ST GERMAIN-BEAUPRÉ

A T the beginning of the eighteenth century the Order had allowed its navy to fall into decay through lack of care and money. Its sailing ships were for the greater part out of commission and for striking power the Order relied on galleys alone, which were light, cheap and at times easy to manage, but more vulnerable than heavier, better armed crafts. In 1700 several shipwrecks compelled the Grand Master to face the fact that such vessels were not the best for waging war at sea. The Mediterranean is a dangerous sea all the year round and it can be deadly in winter, when gales churn the waves into a raging inferno of white foam. In such conditions galleys were unsafe and even at times unmanageable. On February 15, 1700, the Order sustained one of its heaviest losses: that of its leading galley, commanded by Bailly Spinola.

Spinola was cruising off the Sicilian coast when he sighted two ships from Tunis, trying to make their way south through a heavy gale. In spite of the raging wind, Spinola ordered his galley to overtake the enemy but the wind got the better of the Malta vessel. Some of its sails were torn away and disappeared. Even had the galley another set of sails, they could not have been hoisted in the midst of the storm, and the ship could only rely on its oarsmen to overtake the vessel from Tunis. Under such conditions, planning a coherent course was scarcely possible and, as the Malta ship approached its commanding officer realized that it was not responding properly. In fact, when it came near enough to the enemy for boarding it was not responding at all and, striking the Tunis ship, it split open. The last sails came off and fell like a net over the crew. The vessel sank in a few minutes.

Commander Spinola, the Bailly's brother, was killed in the

crash. The Grand Prior of Messina, who was very old and had to lean on his servant's shoulder, fell overboard when the servant was killed, but he was eventually rescued. So was Spinola, the commander of the galley, who had leaped overboard: until the middle of the eighteenth century commanding officers were not obliged to be the last to leave their ships when they had to be abandoned. Another ship of the squadron, the *St Paul* under Commander de Baroncelli-Javon, stood by, impervious to the frightful weather and the increasing danger incurred by remaining stationary in a raging sea. The pilot begged him to row away but he flatly refused, saying that 'he would be too happy to die if he could save but one man of the lost crew'.

How many men were drowned? Reports vary considerably: 150, 500 and even 700 according to letters in the Vatican archives.[1] Bishop Ascanio Bentivoglio, Grand Inquisitor and Ambassador to the Holy See in Malta—those two titles always went together—wrote to Rome, stating that those 700 young men were all under thirty-five and 'the flower of the youth of European nobility'. There were twenty-five Knights among the drowned men: the Chevaliers de Bousseville, Vintimille, Valençay and Villeroy, the latter 'a handsome and well-built lad, who had no taste for his caravans', wrote Saint-Simon, who was his friend and who grieved over his death. It seems that about 160 officers and ranks were saved. The incident was a major tragedy and was mentioned all over Europe in private letters and diplomatic dispatches.

Among those who were missing was Armand Foucald de St Germain de Beaupré. He was twenty and had been for two years in the French navy before going to Malta: his aim was to see service in both navies after the fashion of quite a number of French noblemen. He was the youngest of three brothers, sons of the Marquis de St Germain de Beaupré, an officer in the King's guard, who seems to have been remembered by genealogists mainly for the part he had played when persecuting the Huguenots and destroying their church in Aubusson, where he drove three hundred of them to compulsory conversion.

It took a long time to obtain accurate information about the shipwreck. The south coast of Sicily was difficult to reach and there was a lingering hope that some of the missing men might still be alive, having drifted or swum to safety. The news of the shipwreck had reached Versailles in March and the King had been greatly moved.

The St Germain de Beaupré family were mourning their son and arranging for the third one to go to Malta to replace his drowned brother when a surprising piece of news arrived: the King himself told the Marquis that his son was alive and well. The Minister Pontchartrain had just been notified officially that the young man had been saved. An old friend of the family, G. Vuillard, who had also been an intimate friend of Racine, wrote to one of his correspondents, Louis de Préfontaine: 'The Chevalier de St Germain de Beaupré, twice pushed under the water by an oar which hit him violently on the head, was heaved up and saved by the swell of a wave, under which God's hand was hidden.'[2] He had drifted to the coast, where he was picked up and his wounds attended to. His parents and his grandmother rendered thanks to God that He had spared their progeny.

He was in Italy, still too weak to travel, when news came pouring in, but it was very unreliable. On April 13th Vuillard wrote again to his friend Préfontaine: the situation had changed for the worse. St Germain de Beaupré had died, having been very badly injured by the oars. But he had mercifully found a few days in which to prepare himself for his Creator and his death had been most edifying.

In fact, he did not come to an edifying end until much later, as it happened that the author of the letter had once more accepted a false report. From more reliable sources it was learned that the news of the young man's death was premature. St Germain de Beaupré's skull may have been cracked, but he recovered after having been at death's door. So wrote Vuillard on April 26th. The young man was still in Italy, very frail and slowly recovering from all he had been through; he was not out of danger but had been able to relate to a friend 'the wonderful way in which he had been saved'. At that time Vuillard did not know more. The family were quite exhausted after their nerve-racking experience and anxiously awaited the young Knight, who had written a letter that had been shown to the King.

His return was delayed for several months: he had been very ill indeed and by the beginning of June he was still in Italy. He had probably sustained broken bones and he must have been a powerful swimmer to have made his way to the coast in a raging sea, in spite of wounds and bruises. Early in June he sent to his parents a carefully written account of his ordeal. A friend made copies of it and Vuillard sent one to Préfontaine that has unfortunately been lost.

When at last he was restored to health, St Germain de Beaupré returned home, probably on one of the Order's ships, and abandoned the navy both in France and in Malta. Obviously his experience had been more than enough and, if he had to die fighting, he preferred to do so on terra firma. The next year he entered the French army as a lieutenant in the King's Own Regiment, and in 1702 he joined that unit. He led a very full and very glorious life in the army during the years that followed, fighting in Flanders, Lorraine and Spain, whence he returned loaded with maps for the princes of the royal family. Once more he had refused to die, for there had been a rumour that he had died of small-pox, but the news was false once more.

He was promoted Colonel in 1705. He then met with a set-back when he and his regiment were captured at Ath in Lorraine in 1707. That was the end of his active service. His regiment was re-formed in 1715, and on February 1, 1715, he retired with the rank of Brigadier.[3]

By that time he was just thirty-five: a very early age for retirement, the more so because he was very active, very lively and more intent than ever to taste life to the full. He was given a new opportunity to display his talents and his taste for adventure.

In the spring of 1715 Malta was overcome with fear of war. The reports of spies were the cause. When the Turks started building new ships and increasing their armament, the Order always assumed that they were about to attack the island, to make good their failure of 1565. They never did: it seems that they had been so badly mauled during the Great Siege that they resorted to intimidation by simply making the Order believe that they were about to strike. That is exactly what happened in 1715. Turkish dockyards were turning out ships by the dozen, according to reports from the Order's well-organized intelligence service. The Grand Master, Ramon Perellos, acted accordingly. Fortifications and ships in Valetta had been allowed to decay and rot, mostly through the Grand Master's lack of interest. Perellos had spent large sums of money on tapestries and ornaments: the tapestries were magnificent but the treasury was empty, and when it came to reorganizing the island's defence the only means was by appeal to France, begging for engineers, artillery officers, armourers, guns, ammunition, dockyard equipment, ropes, planks and so on. A tremendously long list of requirements was handed to the Versailles authorities by the Ambassador of the Order. The time was most unpropitious; France was in a terrible financial and military condition, after a long war which had ended in defeat and losses. At most the Grand Master got about one-tenth of what he had asked for.

Meanwhile he had issued a 'call to convent', a sort of general mobilization of all the Knights living on the Continent, whom he summoned to Malta, where they had to report within six months. It was an imperious call and, but for very special and duly authenticated reasons, one could not ignore it. Consequently, a large number of Knights shipped to Valetta, St Germain de Beaupré among them.

The Grand Master was in great terror of impending events; the Knights were quite optimistic. Either they knew more than Perellos or they assumed that nothing was likely to happen, as nothing had ever happened for a century and a half. There was no reason to worry in advance. Besides, February was carnival time and this was one of the great festivals of Malta, lasting not three days but several weeks. It lasted even longer that year, since the company on the island was lively and brilliant, and whether the Grand Master liked it or not they passed their time in the gayest possible fashion. Among visitors who did not belong to the Order, but had come all the same, either to fight or just to do some sight-seeing, was the young Count de Caylus, a keen and scholarly archaeologist. He liked Malta: 'The Knights of all the countries where the Order owns property had gathered there on account of the situation created by the military preparations of the Turks,' he wrote in his account of his journey. 'Consequently the company was good, brilliant and numerous; it was mostly French and there were about 800 lively young men. . . . As far as I could judge, life was far from austere and Malta, at that time, might have been nicknamed Gomorrha Parva.' St Germain de Beaupré was among the Knights who were trying to react actively against boredom, as there was really nothing to do. Caylus had arrived in May, but St Germain had already been there for part of the winter and had had quite enough of it.

The auberges of the Order and the city's inns were filled to capacity and St Germain de Beaupré had to share his lodgings with two young Knights, the Chevalier de Bonel and the Chevalier de Baviére, the latter being obviously a younger son of the Wittelsbach family. Bonel probably came from a Normandy family. St Germain de Beaupré was slightly older than either of them, but he had lost nothing of his youthful spirits.

The Turks did not come, but summer arrived, with its damp heat, drought, dust and sirocco, and by the beginning of June the Grand Master was courteously made to understand that everybody wanted to go home. Besides, he himself wanted to cut down expenses,[4] for the volunteers were draining the Order's resources. Consequently, Perellos allowed the Knights who were in a hurry to leave, according to their expressed desire. St Germaine de Beaupré was among them, together with his two companions, and they decided to travel home through Italy. They hired a boat to take them to Syracuse and left with their servants at midnight on June 7, 1715. Let us quote the comments made by the French Consul in Malta, M. de Canilly, who wrote to the French Secretary of the Navy: 'One wondered why there had never been any gossip about young men of their age and their condition; everybody had been praising their perfect deportment when, on the morning of the 8th, it was discovered that the three young Knights had eloped with one of the loveliest girls in Malta who was barely seventeen; she had run away with them disguised as a boy.'[5]

Obviously, the Consul thought that the whole story was great fun: he was no novice. As for the girl, though she was only seventeen, she was quite adult: Maltese girls, like all women of southern races, mature early and wilt early, too.

It is likely that she had already helped the three young Knights to while away a few tedious hours in Valetta.

On June 18th the French Consul in Naples, the Chevalier de Charlevoix, wrote to Paris: 'The Chevaliers de Baviére, de Bonel and de St Germain de Beaupré have arrived from Malta and have left for Rome.'[6] He did not mention the girl. They duly saw the sights. In July they reached Tuscany. The last episode of their trip is to be found in a third Consular despatch, written by M. de Maillet from Leghorn: 'The Grand Duke and the Princess Dowager of Tuscany are still bestowing tokens of esteem and consideration on the Chevalier de Baviére, who is in Florence with the Chevaliers de Bonel and de St Germain de Beaupré, in spite of the fact that they brought over from Malta a very lovely girl whom they disguised as a boy. The girl has not been heard of in Naples, Rome or Florence.'[7]

It is possible that the lovely Maltese girl had found in Naples a single lover, richer than the three young Knights who had clubbed together to provide for their mistress. The story had not been kept secret and the various Consuls had relished it. What is stranger is the fact that it had been duly appreciated at the court of the Grand Duke of Tuscany. Cosimo III was ludicrously ugly, very old, very bigoted and completely senile. He had emptied his treasury to pay for his demented religious hobbies. Had he heard of the Maltese girl he would have been horrified. The reason why this episode had been related at court may have been the close family connection between the Chevalier de Baviére and the Dowager Princess, Violante of Bavaria, Cosimo's daughter-in-law and the widow of his elder son, Ferdinand. He had never been able to bear her, as she was very plain. After his death she kept her own court and basked in the affection of her brother-in-law, Gian-Gastone.

What happened next to the pleasant trio is unknown. St Germain de Beaupré returned to France. It seems that the Order of Malta had resented his leaving the navy after the shipwreck. He was passed over for promotion many times and was not made a Commander until 1746, when he was sixty-six. He was then granted the Commandery of Abbeville. In 1755 he was made Grand Prior of Aquitaine, one of the three Grand Priories of the Langue de France. Though he was old at the time, he was able to enjoy his new dignities for several years, since he did not die until 1767, at the ripe age of eighty-seven, having survived his shipwreck for sixty-seven years.

CHAPTER VIII

SLAVES IN ALGIERS

~❧❀❧~

IN 1707 Oran, then a Spanish territory of North Africa, was besieged by the Turks. Leaning against a mountain range, the Murdjajo, which commands a large, well-sheltered harbour, the town was practically impregnable; but the garrison and the officers were so poor that the enemy had a reasonable hope of overrunning the city. The Governor, Don Gregorio Caraffa, a Knight of Malta, was less than incompetent. No help could be expected from Spain: Philip V was fighting in Europe against an increasing number of enemies and his assistance was hardly more than moral. The situation became so dangerous that eventually the Order was asked to come to the help of the beleaguered.

This was quite in keeping with the Order's mission. The Knights of St John had sworn to fight against the Infidel always and anywhere, and Grand Master Perellos therefore granted the King of Spain's request. The Chevalier de Langon, one of the Order's best sailors, was put in charge of the fleet and everything went wrong. One of his officers, the Chevalier de St Pierre, did succeed in landing 350 men at Oran by July 1, 1707, but for some unknown reason the Governor made himself thoroughly unpleasant to his colleagues from Malta, and Langon complained bitterly of his unbearable lack of courtesy and initiative. It was as if the man had a grudge against the Order and had made up his mind to make them pay heavily for the help they brought to the city. On leaving Oran Langon ran into a squadron of Turkish ships and captured one of them, which he found laden with gunpowder. He brought it back to Oran, and it was a godsend for a beleaguered city; but Langon was scarcely thanked and he left in a towering rage.

The Knights of Malta were detailed to defend two fortresses

to the south of the city, St Andrew and St Philip, overlooking the deep ravine of Raz-el-Ain. They fought hard and with great courage, while the Spanish garrison stood by, hoping that things would end quickly as they had had more than enough of a desultory fight. On September 22nd a mine blew up in Fort St Philip and forty men were captured, thirty of whom were wounded. Among the latter were two French Knights, Laurent de Vento de Pennes, whose right arm was broken, and Boniface de Castellane d'Esparron, whose cheek had been torn open by a musket shot. Suddenly, news came that the Governor had surrendered and had hurried back to Spain with his family while the garrison retired to Mers-el-Kebir.[1]

On February 4, 1708, one of the Order's servants at arms, Mathieu Beaulme, wrote to Grand Master Perellos to give him an account of what had happened. 'Two or three Maltese have been sold;[2] as for ourselves, we are most rigorously watched. The Christians retreated from Oran on January 20th and the Captain-General retreated to Los Alcaras,[3] whence he ran away the next day. Fort St Andrew surrendered the same day, but we do not know under what conditions.'[4] Among the prisoners sold into slavery were the two wounded Knights, de Pennes and de Castellane, though they had been promised the honours of war, Beaulme himself and an Italian Knight named Balbani. The situation of the Christian slaves in Algiers was hardly less distressing than at the time when Cervantes had been a captive there in the sixteenth century: the Arabs always treat a captive enemy with the most repulsive cruelty, and the four Knights were wounded, exhausted men, who had fought hard under disheartening conditions. Furthermore, Maltese Knights underwent the worst treatment because they were dangerous enemies and had been taken only after the most desperate resistance. Their ransoms were set at the highest level because they were thought to be rich, which was not the case. In fact, Castellane was extremely poor: he had nine brothers and sisters, all of whom were in Malta or in religious orders.

Several months elapsed and by the end of June, 1708, Vento de Pennes wrote to the Grand Master to thank him for the regular payment of their pensions. He and his three companions were in good health and the outlook was not too grim, as they were hoping to be ransomed fairly soon; but days and weeks passed and the change was for the worse. The scorching Algerian summer came and went; no ransom was forthcoming and the gaolers began to increase the pressure. Vento de Pennes wrote again, merely stating facts, as one gentleman writing to another: he could not demean himself by stressing his point too heavily: 'They have chained us and brought us out of the Christians' prison. We are now working day and night in the harbour, though there were orders that we should not be compelled to work.' Monks who specialized in ransoming slaves had come and had given them some money from the Grand Master. Their ransoms had been put at 4,000 piastres each.[5]

The monks started bargaining with the Arabs. One feels that they might have been buying cattle, for the lack of human interest they displayed. The monks continued their negotiations for months, trying to outplay the Arabs, who were masters of the game. Then they decided to restrict themselves to ransoming the women and children, and finally broke off all negotiations.[6] There was a lively display of ill-will on both side. As for the King of Spain, he stated at once that he had no money to buy back men who had volunteered to help him and had lost their freedom in his service. Hope therefore lay in Perellos alone.

Meanwhile, the Grand Master had received a letter which would have made some impression on a less hardened mind. It had been written by the father of one of the slaves, Nicholas de Pennes, Marquess of Perusse. It ran thus: 'My son, the Chevalier, having been happy enough to save the Order's flag at the siege of Oran, and being unable to present it in person to Your Most Serene Highness, as he is held captive in Algiers, I am entrusting the Chevalier de Lacépède with it. Had not my great age prevented me from doing so, I would have had the honour to bring it in person and bow to Your Most Serene Highness. . . .'

He added nothing about the tragic life of his son in his Algerian prison. Nothing developed and it is quite likely that Perellos was not in the least moved by the letter, which he did not even answer. It was simply endorsed with the words:

'Received March 15, 1708'.

On December 6th, Vento de Pennes wrote again: women and children had at last been ransomed and the monks were to start negotiations for the captive Spanish officers, including the Knights of Malta. By that time Louis XIV had heard of the business and had written to his grandson, Philip V, to inquire into the matter.[8] Then silence fell for two years.

Meanwhile, the French Consul in Algiers, M. de Clérambault, had made contact with the captives and proved to be their only active, intelligent and compassionate friend. Their situation was becoming intolerable. An Algerian ship had been captured at sea by the Bailly de Langon and the Dey of Algiers was incensed. As a reprisal he had chained the four Knights and had shut them up in a repulsive dungeon, where they remained for several months, until Vento de Pennes managed to get a message to the Consul to tell him of their plight. Clérambault called on the Dey at once, stormed and threatened until the latter gave way and agreed to let the four men out of their living tomb. They were then given better accommodation and lighter chains. A few months later, the Consul married: his bride was a Mlle Durant, his predecessor's sister. His wedding provided him with an opportunity to try and help the captives. He called on the Dey once more and in a most formal way told him of his marriage and begged permission to ask the four captives to the ceremony and the feast which was to follow. Permission was granted and the Knights' chains were struck off. They could wash, shave and dress in decent European clothes, probably provided by the Consular staff. The wedding was very gay and they were happy, back for a while in civilized surroundings.

There had been some talk of their being exchanged for men of the captured ship, and the future looked a little less dismal when, in the very middle of the party, their hopes were dashed. A Turk, recently freed from Malta, arrived with the news that Turkish prisoners in the island had been tortured and compelled to renounce their religion. Moreover, the Grand Master had flatly refused any exchange of prisoners: he hypocritically wrote to Clérambault that the slaves were not his, but the Order's. The Dey immediately had the four Knights brought back. They were summoned in the middle of the feast, and with tears in their eyes they undressed, took off their wigs, re-assumed their dirty prison garb and surrendered to their gaolers.

Clérambault's young wife was in tears and the Consul shared her sorrow.[9] He thought at once of some new way to save them. In February 1711 he wrote to the Grand Master to tell him how unwise his attempt at persecuting the Turks had been: 'The Knights have been sent down to work with the other slaves. They were carrying stones. . . . The work would have quickly put them beyond any need of ransom, especially the Chevalier Balbani, who was frailer than the rest, and was exhausted by the second day. They stopped work then, except for the Chevalier de Pennes, who was kept for three more days, dragging a cart.'[10] Vento de Pennes was supposed to have asked Perellos to put pressure on the Turkish slaves but Clérambault thought this highly improbable: 'For the two whole months during which the Chevalier de Vento de Pennes lived in my house, I saw him so much adverse to any idea of having the Turkish slaves ill-treated that I can only ascribe that report to sheer malice,' he wrote.[11] And he went on to request the Grand Master to inquire into the matter. Perellos did nothing of the sort; in fact, he did nothing at all.

On April 23, 1711, two months after they had been sent back to their prison, Vento de Pennes and Castellane d'Esparron jointly signed a letter to Perellos. It is tragic but dignified: 'For four years we have languished in chains in Algiers, and we have refrained from worrying Your Eminence with our sorrows. . . . The Brothers of Mercy have come and have refused to help us, either with their own money or the King's: they said that we were rich,' they wrote. They had believed in the Grand Master's charity and they had been cruelly deceived. They continued: 'We very humbly implore you to consider the fact that we are in great trouble merely because we obeyed promptly the orders of our generals. We did not hesitate to sacrifice ourselves and we take the liberty to remind you that we would not have displayed such blind obedience had we not believed that the prince we were serving was too generous to abandon the wretched men who had lost everything in his service.' Their families were to attempt to ransom them; as for themselves, they had already mortgaged their pensions. The Grand Master had forsaken them and they had lost hope.[12]

Perellos waited until July 27th before replying, and his letter, brutal and full of hypocrisy, was certainly hurtful to the captives. 'We have received your letter of April 23rd in which we have been very sorry to read of the deplorable state you are in,' he wrote. . . . 'We could have wished to see you less prostrate and more resigned to God's will.' Perellos reminded them that their pensions did not belong to them and could not be mortgaged. He suggested that they should appeal to their families for help, as he could do nothing.[13]

He had found a secure basis: advocating a religious conception of life is always easy and sometimes effective when one tries to reprove someone for his lack of compliance to God's will. If he attempts to deny the charge, he can be taxed with pride and the matter is dropped. Yet it is sickening to see a man, living in the comfort and splendour of the Maltese palaces, reproving captives for their refusing to remain in slavery indefinitely. This Algerian episode vexed Perellos and he was trying to shift the responsibility on to everyone but himself. Immediately after the surrender of Oran he had written to Pontchartrain, Louis XIV's minister: 'As for the capture of Oran, it should not be ascribed to the late arrival of our ships. I sent them as soon as they could put out to sea. . . . The loss of the city is even more painful to me, as several of my Knights and one of my subjects have lost their liberty, and I have no means to redeem them, if His Majesty does not help them out of pity and kindness.'[14] Perellos had made up his mind and decided to do nothing.

Meanwhile, the French Consul in Algiers was doing everything in his power to help the four poor men. The Dey, in his view, was not at heart a wicked man, and Clérambault secured permission to keep the Chevalier Balbani, who was still very ill, in his own house. The Chevalier had been badly treated because his uncle was a Grand Cross of the Order. His three companions were still in the common prison.

Another year elapsed. France was quarrelling with the Barbary States, and the Ambassador of the Order in Paris, the Bailly de la Vieuville, was wondering about the fate of the captives, should Louis XIV break with Algiers. 'The freeing of the enslaved Knights would be delayed until a very distant future,' he wrote.[15] But Perellos had decided to drop the matter altogether, by entrusting it to Louis XIV's tender mercy, and as the King had known the whole story since 1708 and had done nothing it was likely that nothing would happen in the future.

In January 1713 he wrote to the King, requesting his help for the Chevalier d'Esparron, whose brother Gaspard, also a Knight of Malta, was going to Versailles; he begged the King to find some means to free the brother who was in Algiers, 'in a narrow prison, chained and closely watched', and could not be ransomed by the Order. Perellos, who had never been interested hitherto in the young man's fate, was now trying to enlist the King's interest.[16] By the same post, and in the same words, he wrote to his Ambassador in Paris, introducing the younger d'Esparron, who was intending to go to Versailles. Then Perellos felt relieved, hoping he was now rid of the tiresome affair.

The interview with the younger d'Esparron must have been distressing: Gaspard de Castellane d'Esparron was an officer in the Royal Army and a Gentleman of the Bedchamber to the Duke of Orleans. He was able to secure help at court. It seems that some efforts were made at Versailles to find a solution, but it was slow work. By the middle of 1714 it was suggested once more that the Grand Master might exchange some of the 210 Barbary slaves for the four Knights. The French Consul in Malta—the 'King's man'—the Chevalier de Montmorency Laval, discussed the matter and Perellos flatly refused, using his former argument: the slaves were not his property, but the Order's, and such an exchange would create a dangerous precedent.[17] Laval was indignant but Perellos was obstinate. By March the Consul was still quite unsuccessful. He was deeply moved by the four men's fate: he had had news of them three months earlier. Perellos constantly repeated his argument that they had their pensions and could use them to ransom themselves. He became tearful, spoke of his love for them and of his charity, but refused to squander on them the money which should be bestowed on the poor. Of course, if the King insisted, if he gave strict orders, it might be different.[18] The King did nothing. His hardness and lack of sentiment are well known and he was not interested anyway. The spring and the summer of 1715 elapsed. Then on September 1st Louis XIV died and Philip of Orleans became Regent.

The situation changed at once. While Perellos was hoping that the whole thing was shelved at last, a letter from the newly-appointed Ambassador in Paris, the Bailly de Mesmes, arrived and shattered his hard-won peace. On December 6, 1715, while the Regent was thought to be completely engrossed in the new financial scheme put forward to him by John Law of Lauriston, he had found time to summon the Ambassador to the Palais Royal and hand him a letter for the Grand Master about the four enslaved Knights. The Ambassador's own letter was as follows:

'Until now, despite any request to me to beg for their ransom, and in spite of my own ardent wish to help them, I have been careful not to forget that the Order's regulations forbid me to meddle with such problems. I therefore waited until the Regent spoke to me about the matter. The friends and relatives of those poor Knights have had access to the Prince and have told him of their sad situation after a long period of slavery. Moved by well-deserved pity, the Duke of Orleans spoke to me in a very pressing way and suggested I should approach Your Highness on the subject, putting forward the fact that it would please him greatly if you could ignore the various considerations which have hitherto prevented you from putting an end to their slavery. The kingdom hopes for, and looks forward to, their liberation with great anxiety.'[19]

The matter was put so forcibly that Perellos could not pretend not to have understood: this was an order. He could not procrastinate nor make a show of religious eloquence; he could only obey. The Regent's letter is lost, but it is easy to imagine how it was worded. Together with many faults and a few vices, Philip of Orleans had several virtues, including energy and mercy. Having made up his mind, he did not allow the matter to drag, or Perellos to hush it up. Three days after writing a first letter, Mesmes had to write another, after a second summons to the Palais Royal. The Regent demanded an immediate answer: 'He was greatly moved by the plight of the enslaved Knights,' Mesmes wrote, 'and he expects Your Highness to act at once.'[20]

The money which for years had been impossible to find was forthcoming at once and Clérambault was instructed to reopen negotiations and this time to succeed. On June 30, 1716, Beaulme arrived at Marseille and wrote a respectful but curt letter to the Grand Master to thank him for his recovered liberty. He had been ransomed for 2,200 piastres, the Knights for 100 more. The Grand Master maintained their pensions. When bargaining had begun, the Knights had been priced at 4,000 piastres each. Had they been so badly treated and were they so exhausted that their commercial value had been almost halved? It seems very likely.

It is impossible to discover what became of Balbani. Castellane d'Esparron left the Order, securing release from his vows: a not very surprising decision. He entered the French army and became a Brigadier-General. In 1745 he married Renée Fournier and had two daughters, though he was no longer young. As for Vento de Pennes, he remained in France for several months, then went back to Malta; he took with him a letter from Mesmes, commending him to the Grand Master: 'His services and the long spell in captivity which he has suffered are enough to rouse your magnanimous pity,' wrote the Ambassador.[21] If Perellos, who was now very old and quite senile, was able to understand the letter, he may have found in it some bitter, if involuntary, irony.

At about the same time, Mesmes begged the Grand Master to make a grant to Beaulme, and recommended him to Cellamare, the Spanish Ambassador in Paris, in the hope he could be given some employment in Spain.[22] His subsequent career was brilliant. He was made a Commander and he entered the Emperor's service. He reached the rank of colonel, governed Broden in Hungary and before 1750 had retired and settled in Burgundy, near Mâcon. For years he was a sick man, always about to recover and never recovering fully. It is possible that some disease, contracted in Algiers, developed in old age. He made the acquaintance of one of his Malta colleagues, Commander de Monts de Savasse, who lived near him and very kindly looked after him.

In November 1765 he visited the old man, who was on the

point of death, and wrote to one of his Malta colleagues:

'I went to Mâcon on the 15th . . . and visited Commander Beaulme at once. He grabbed my hand with considerable strength and said many things of which I did not catch a word, neither did his three servants, as he roared like thunder; I stayed with him for more than four hours, during which he got three times out of bed to sit near the fire. On my arrival I told him that, having heard he was ill, I had come to give him back the four *louis* I owed him and to offer him any help he might desire. . . . His servants put the money into his purse and the purse into the pocket of his dressing-gown. He smoked a pipe and drank several cups of broth, and seeing he had still some strength left, I did not wish to hurt him by having his properties sealed. . . . He had only a few garments fit for an invalid, and they were dirty and stank worse than a pig sty, so I thought it superfluous to have them sealed up, as one could touch his belongings only with tongs and with gloves on.'[23]

A few days later Beaulme died and Monts de Savasse wrote again:

'Tonight I heard that Commander Beaulme, who has been con-valescing for about twenty years, was despaired of and had been given the Sacraments. Being unable to go to him at night because of the wretched weather, I sent my seal to the notary . . . to have it put on the poor belongings of the Commander, which are locked in his wardrobe and chest, together with his stores of cheese, salted preserves and such choice delicacies, and to let me know at once if he should die during the night.'[24]

It is likely that Beaulme had got into the habit of keeping all his stores under lock and key while he was a slave and had to be careful to save every scrap of food.

The man who emerged best from the whole sad story is the Regent. He never lost his interest in the men whose lives he had obviously saved. Much later, in 1755, his grandson wrote to another Grand Master, Pinto de Fonseca, to introduce another Chevalier de Vento de Pennes, Henri, who was twenty-six: 'In 1717, His Royal Highness the Regent, my grandfather, wrote to Grand Master Perellos on behalf of the Chevalier de Pennes, this young man's uncle, who had endured harsh captivity in Barbary.'[25] The Orleans had not forgotten.

In 1720 Perellos was dead. He had been buried in the magnificent Church of St John in Valetta. On his tomb a pupil of Bernini had carved two lovely statues: Justice and Charity.

Tomb of the Grand Master de Rohan
in St John's, Valetta

Tomb of the Grand Master de Vilhena

Sixteenth-century Italian print of the Siege of Malta; Jean de la
Valette in the middle of his troops

L'ASSALTO GENERALE ALLA POSTA DI CASTIGLIA ADI XXI DI AGOSTO MDLXV

Chevalier d'Aydie (by an unknown painter)

7. Commander Gabriel Dubois de la Ferté

CHAPTER IX

THE DUC DE SAINT-SIMON'S COUSIN

꘎꘎꘎

THE Duc de Saint-Simon, the author of the fascinating *Memoirs* which bring the courts of Louis XIV and the Regent so vividly to life, had a large, impoverished and unmanageable family. A distant cousin of his father, Titus de Rouvroy de Saint-Simon, died in 1712 and Saint-Simon's comment was: 'He and his father had obscurely devoured more than 40,000 *livres* without setting foot outside their estates.'

When Titus died he left a widow with four sons, a daughter and no money. The daughter married an Auvergne nobleman, the Marquis de la Richardie, and we shall hear more about her in another chapter. Two of her brothers had entered the Church. The other two were in the army. Saint-Simon, when he went to Spain as an ambassador, took two of his cousins with him. But not the youngest; that one, Claude de Rouvroy de Saint-Simon, was going to lead a most eventful life.

He was born in 1694 and his family decided that he should be a monk. He had no choice, and while still a boy was clapped into an Augustin monastery, the St Victor Abbey in Paris: it stood on the site of the present Jardin des Plantes and the Halle aux Vins, near the Seine. Without any religious vocation whatever, Claude was obliged to assume the habit of the order and take his vows, filled with helpless rage all the time. Yet he resisted as far as he could and in 1713, when he was nineteen, he begged to be allowed to obtain a transfer into the Order of Malta. Though not very old, his family had the required quarters of nobility to allow him to do so and he could muster the necessary help at court. On January 26, 1714, Louis XIV wrote to his Ambassador in Rome, Cardinal de la Tremoille: 'M. de Saint-Simon, canon regular of the Order of St Augustin, professing monk of the St Victor Abbey in Paris, has put to me that, as he rightly wishes to join the Order of Malta, he requires a Papal brief. . . . The Duc de Saint-Simon has also begged for my help in the matter and I have condescended to grant him my protection. My will is that you second him with all your power and in my name.'

In spite of that powerful protection, the Pope refused the young man permission to leave his Order. It is not known why his feelings were so strong that he chose to resist the French king's wish. Anyhow, Claude de Saint-Simon broke down. He could not bear the thought of spending his life in that dull, drab place: it was unthinkable, and the young man simply refused to waste his life in that way. He managed to secure lay clothes and money, escaped from his monastery and rode out of Paris to freedom. Freedom meant England, which he soon reached, in the seventeenth and the eighteenth century the shelter of runaway laymen and priests. It is easy to imagine the frantic fury of Claude's family when they heard the news.

Having safely crossed the Channel, the young man settled into ordinary life—probably a gay one. He married and, according to a family tradition, begat two children, but nothing is known about his activities and even his wife's name has not survived. He lived in England for several years, but in 1720 came a change: he had probably run out of money and could not borrow more. What became of his wife and children is not known, but Claude de Saint-Simon went back to France and was arrested as soon as he landed, as his mother had been granted a *lettre de cachet* to bring the black sheep back to the fold. The letter allowed her to have her son arrested and detained at the King's pleasure—what is nowadays called *internement administratif*, though it takes place in less comfortable conditions. While Claude was first in his monastery and then in England, on the strength of his vow of poverty his relatives had pounced on his meagre inheritance.

He was brought back to his mother's house in Paris, as she had been made his keeper, but he did not yield to such an outrage. He started a lawsuit against his mother and his eldest brother. (The latter was painted by Rigaud and his portrait is now in the Grenoble Museum: the man looks sly and thoroughly unappealing.) Claude sought redress for having been compelled to make his vows against his will, and also for the loss of his inheritance. The Duc de Saint-Simon himself intervened: he did not trust the youngest son and he did not want him to make things more difficult than they already were for Mme de Saint-Simon. Claude heard of his cousin's attitude and in his anger foolishly stated in front of witnesses that, should he lose his suit, he would smash the skull of his eldest brother and of his cousin. Here is a contemporary account of the episode, written by President Mathieu Marais:

'The Officialty had judged the case of the Marquis de Saint-Simon, who was contesting his vows, made at the Abbey of St Victor. The vows are valid, and as he has boasted that he would kill his brother and the Duc his relative, he has been arrested near Notre-Dame, on a *lettre de cachet* delivered against him, kidnapped and carried to the Fort de Joux. He had run away from St Victor and escaped to England, where he had not behaved like a well-balanced man. He is a bad lot, like all runaway monks. He has been firmly dealt with and that is right.'

Marais was neither compassionate nor imaginative. The young Marquess was taken to Joux in the dead of winter, and it is easy to imagine how unpleasant the place was. It is an old fortress, powerfully fortified in the seventeenth century, at the top of a high rock, in the very middle of the pass which leads from Pontarlier to Neuchâtel, one of the coldest and most windy places in Europe. The wind howls round it, piling the snow high or shrouding the place in a raging white inferno. The accommodation was more than primitive. The view is dreary: forests of dark fir trees and flat expanses of snow-covered fields and marshes, or bogs.

The young man felt completely crushed. Everything had turned against him and he was facing a blank wall. Going back over his past, he felt he was more unlucky than guilty—except towards his wife; he also realized that he must ingratiate himself with those who had broken him but who yet might save him. What he did is not known, but he obviously approached his cousin, begging for his forgiveness. Saint-Simon, despite his fiery temper, was generous and a man of honour. He reacted well and quickly to his cousin's entreaties and wrote to the Grand Master of Malta, Marcantonio Zondadari, a letter which is in the Valetta Archives:

'M. de Saint-Simon, who belongs to the elder branch of my house and who has been for a short while a Canon regular of the Order of St Augustin and a professing monk at the Abbey of St Victor in Paris, has strong reasons for requesting Your Highness's graceful permission to be transferred into the Order of Malta as a professing Knight of Justice. I would feel guilty of a gross lack of the veneration due to the illustrious head of such an august militia, should my name come under his eyes unaccompanied by my most humble request, together with the enclosed statement of the case. This only to show him my profound respect as I cannot think that anything can be added to the letter of introduction the King has been pleased to grant. Trusting in it, I earnestly beg Your Eminence to be so kind as to listen favourably to the reasons put to him, and I trust more in your kindness and your consideration for His Majesty's wish than in anything else. If there is anything that could plead for me in the present situation, I can truthfully state that it would be my passionate admiration for an Order so useful to Christianity and my respect for Your Eminence and for the august body of which he is the head.'[1]

The letter is undated but its position in the file of the Grand Master's correspondence suggests the spring of 1721. Saint-Simon was the Regent's devoted friend and Philip of Orleans had a gift for friendship. He had the whole matter put to him and, on June 28, 1721, he wrote to the Grand Master reminding him that he would be grieved if he turned down his request on behalf of the young Marquess 'who has an ardent wish to serve the religion in his Order; so does his family, for whom I have a special affection'. He then asked the Grand Master to make things easy for Saint-Simon, adding that he knew it might be difficult but that something should be done for the scion of so noble a family, hinting at the fact that 'I am willing to give you proofs of my affection any time there is an opportunity to do so'.[2]

Difficult it certainly was! One of the oaths sworn by a professing Knight of Malta was that he had never belonged to any other Order, and young Saint-Simon was an Augustin monk! A few days after Philip of Orleans' letter, the Ambassador of the Order in Paris, the Bailly des Mesmes, wrote to the Grand Master (August 6, 1721). He had seen the Regent several times and it was obvious that the latter would do much to help his friend's cousin. The Order had every reason to welcome a Saint-Simon: his family was sufficiently old and enjoyed the Regent's favour. Accepting Claude de Saint-Simon would mean enlisting the Duc's influence in the service of the Order and that could be very useful just then, for the Order had sustained heavy losses when John Law's financial schemes had collapsed. The Common Treasury had been badly drained, and most of the French Knights had been ruined. So Mesmes suggested that the Grand Master should yield at once, as graciously as possible, not trying to shift the responsibility on Rome.[3] Zondadari understood and acted accordingly. On October 5th he wrote to Philip of Orleans, stating that 'he was granting that singular, unprecedented grace' to the Marquess de Saint-Simon. He trusted that his cousin 'would use his influence to help us to receive a yearly grant so necessary to enable our Order to honour its promises'.[4] It was clearly a matter of give and take. Claude de Saint-Simon was granted his wish and the Order secured its grant.

Back to freedom and semi-secular life, Saint-Simon did not hurry to Malta: there was no need to do so now that all was clear. He lingered at Court and he made his vows in Paris by special permission. In 1729 he was still vaguely contemplating the idea of travelling south to join the Order in earnest. Apparently he pleaded his difficult family situation to delay his coming. His mother was dead and his cousin was now his staunch friend. In Malta, Zondadari had died. The next Grand Master, Manoel Vilhena, wrote, hoping that M. de Saint-Simon would be at last free to come and serve the Order.

In 1730 the Pope died, there was a conclave and Saint-Simon went to Rome as assistant to the Cardinal de Rohan. After the election he posted south and arrived in Malta. He had made a melodramatic scene in Rome, throwing himself at the feet of the newly-elected Pope, sobbing and explaining that he and his family were destitute—which was true—and begging that, as soon as he was in Malta, he should be given a galley. The Pope probably could not have cared less and therefore granted everything. So Saint-Simon came to the Grand Master with most urgent orders and he got his galley quickly. Several of his rivals were very jealous, the Chevalier de Monts de Savasse among them.[5]

In 1732, back in France, he sent the Grand Master a papal order that he should be made a Grand Cross: it was unprecedented and Vilhena was becoming rather weary of the Chevalier de Saint-Simon and his affairs. He implored the Ambassador to make the Chevalier realize that the rank could not be granted to a Knight who would only assume his command at sea within the next four months: a Grand Cross would give him the rank above a General, which was unthinkable. He promptly added that this was not a refusal: just a request not to hasten matters too much. The Ambassador used the Duc to break the news to his cousin. So Claude de Saint-Simon went to Malta and assumed command of his ship. He proved an excellent officer and once saved his galley in a raging gale. In 1735 he was made a General of the Galleys and was granted the Grand Cross; he received various commands and was provoted to the rank of Bailly in 1736: he was then forty years of age.

Even then Claude de Saint-Simon was far from rich. His naval commands had got him heavily into debt; the commanderies he had been given were not very fine ones and in 1739 his cousin wrote an indignant letter to the Ambassador, the Bailly de Mesmes, whom he hated, but he managed to remain polite:

'After what has happened to the promise you were kind enough to make to the Bailly de Saint-Simon, that he would be handsomely rewarded for all he spent serving the Religion as a captain and then as a general of the galleys, I hope you will kindly write to the Grand Master, stating how right we are to complain of the excessive number of pensions to be paid out of the income of the Commandery he has just been granted. I know it well, for it is within a league of here and it does not bring in half of what it is accounted for. I then beg you most forcibly to do us a service. . . .'

He added below his signature:

'All my respects to M. d'Ambers. I warn you, both of you, that the weather here is more than glorious, but I am speaking to deaf men, engulfed in the turmoil of life at court and in Paris, who will not come for a rest in Brie.'[6]

Claude de Saint-Simon went again to Malta and came back in 1743, when he was warmly welcomed at Court. He had become a member of the small and rather dull group which attended the Queen. Marie Leczinska was neither young nor beautiful, and she had never been very bright. She liked Saint-Simon, she recommended him to the Grand Master when he went to Malta, she played cards with him when he came back, and she danced with him. The Duc de Luynes, one of the best memoir writers of that time, described them dancing a minuet 'very tolerably'. Saint-Simon was granted the envied right to drive in the Queen's coaches. He was given a small apartment in Fontainebleau, and another in Versailles, very high up in the Aile des Princes—the left wing when facing the park. At Marly, where the selection of inmates was even more exclusive, he was not officially included, but pleasantly tolerated. He was about fifty, a man of great mien, of good culture and some means at last. He had settled down to a quiet, dignified life. He was in constant attendance on the King and also on Mme de Pompadour, in spite of his friendship with the Queen. When, in 1749, Louis XV wanted to have his cousin Conti appointed Grand Prior of France against Grand Master Pinto's wish, it was Saint-Simon who did all he could to have the King's wish gratified.

The Duc de Saint-Simon had died in 1755, to the great sorrow of his cousin, who had been his staunch friend for many years. Suddenly, in November 1757, Saint-Simon called on everybody at Court in great haste, taking leave of the King and Queen and departing practically overnight: 'He had been summoned to Malta by several Grand Crosses who dreaded the election of the Bailly de Tencin. The Grand Master is not yet dead,' wrote Luynes, who had been present at the farewell audience. No, Pinto was not yet dead, and he went on living for fifteen years more! Saint-Simon had arrived Malta in a rage and then had to kick his heels on the island, feeling bored and foolish. To soothe him, Pinto sent him as Ambassador to

Naples, and then after a few seasons there or at Ischia, a fashionable Spa, he drifted back to Versailles.

Pinto died at last in 1772, and Saint-Simon was now officially competing for his succession, sparing neither effort nor money. He again hurried back to Valetta. The Grand Inquisitor Manciforte who, as he represented the Holy See in Malta, was on very bad terms with the Order, like all his predecessors and successors, ferreted out every disparaging episode, and among others discovered that Saint-Simon had given 8,000 *scudi* to a Swiss Knight, Pfyffer vonWeir, 400 to Commander Frederico Tedesco and to Commander Erera, and small sums to others, to secure their votes.[7] But his rival, Ximenes y Texada, paid more and was eventually elected, and he proved to be one of the worst Grand Masters ever.

As an act of appeasement Saint-Simon was appointed Ambassador to Paris and he hurried back to France. On March 20, 1773, he made his solemn entry first into Paris and then into Versailles, greeted by the King, the Dauphin Louis, the Dauphine Marie-Antoinette and Mesdames. His old friend the Queen had died. As a member of the diplomatic corps, he had all the other Ambassadors calling at his house in the rue de la Ville l'Evêque: the Nuncio, the Ambassadors from Spain, Savoy, Denmark, Russia, England, the Netherlands and Saxony, envoys from Genoa, Cologne and many others.[8] Though Saint-Simon was now quite an old man, he was still active and very popular.

In 1775 Ximenes died but Saint-Simon was too old to hurry back to Malta. Besides, he had no hope whatever of being elected. His rival was Emmanuel de Rohan, a clever, active, generous man of fifty. Saint-Simon remained in Versailles, calling on the young King in great state to notify him of the Grand Master's death. He and his assistants wore black dress and stockings, with silver swords and buckles, he reported in a letter to the new Grand Master.[9] He represented the Order at Louis XVI's coronation in Reims.

He lived until 1777. He was buried in Paris in one of the Order's churches, Ste Marie du Temple. In Malta his friends erected a monument to his memory in the Chapel of France in St John: it is one of the beautiful mosaic slabs, representing Death pulling down the Bailly's bust while Time tries to keep it erect. The bust must be of Claude de Saint-Simon himself. So ended a varied and tempestuous life, so fitting to a member of the Rouvroy Saint-Simon family.

CHAPTER X

AN ENVOY EXTRAORDINARY
TO ENGLAND

JOESPH DE MONTMORENCY-LAVAL

❧❦❧

ONTACTS between the Order of Malta and England
were not very frequent but when they did take place
the Order was careful to behave with the greatest
courtesy in order to ingratiate itself with a leading sea-power
whose ships were constantly passing through the Mediterranean. Officially there had been no relations since 1560,
though the Order had never been suppressed in England and,
with a good deal of realism, Grand Masters tried to be as
pleasant as possible towards English sovereigns. It was most
necessary since otherwise things might have been very difficult. Maltese pirates grabbed anything at sea, including
English, or English-protected vessels, which was illegal. When
England was at war her enemies, usually Spain, sold English
prizes in Valetta and that was even more illegal, as the Order
was obliged to be neutral towards Christian princes. There
was a so-called English consul in Valetta, but the Grand
Master did not acknowledge Protestants and the various
people who held the post were so incompetent and shady that
neither England nor the Grand Master trusted them. Such a
situation did not make things easy.

A crisis developed in 1713. English sailors complained that
they had been ill-treated in Malta; at the same time an English
ship was seized and brought to Valetta to be sold. The matter
could have been easily settled had there been some reliable
person with whom to discuss it, but there was no one on the
spot. Nevertheless, something might be done by very circui-
tous means: the Order's Ambassador in Paris, the Bailly de la
Vieuville, was instructed to call on his English colleague to

see what could be done. That colleague was the poet Matthew Prior.

According to Saint-Simon, La Vieuville was quite a gentleman, as noble and generous as could be in his office, without harming anybody. When he called on Prior the two men took a great liking to each other. In Malta, the Grand Master Perellos was quite out of his depth: he had realized too late what had happened and he did not understand the problem. He explained the whole matter in a perfectly honest letter to Admiral Jennings and also to Queen Anne.[1] In Paris, La Vieuville and Prior went over the whole matter together and the former wrote to Perellos in June, telling him that 'the Minister (Prior) is a great gentleman and has been most gracious to me'. He had tried to explain to Prior the Order's shaky neutrality and how very sorry they were that something had gone wrong.[2] La Vieuville also met the Duke of Shrewsbury, but he dealt mostly with Prior. He was also worried by another matter: why the Queen did not answer the Grand Master's letter. Perellos was greatly dismayed, but he received an explanation from Paris: his letter had duly arrived in Whitehall, but no one knew how to address a Grand Master, and Prior had been instructed to inquire in Versailles about the correct procedure.[3] The English minister also thought of completely reorganizing the consular service in Valetta, which made the Grand Master shudder.

Early in January 1714 the two Ambassadors met again and Prior was more charming than ever. He told La Vieuville that the Queen's letter would arrive very soon and, in fact, he handed it to his colleague on January 22nd.[4] It was in Latin. (Charles II had writen to the Order in English and James II in French.) The letter was most formal and respectful and it might have been a good beginning for a resumption of negotiations when everything broke down again at once. La Vieuville had to abandon his diplomatic work to be cut for stone; he did not survive the operation. Queen Anne died of a stroke shortly afterwards and the new government recalled Prior to England. Everything came to a standstill.

Everything except the obnoxious Maltese pirates—the new King's enemies. One could expect trouble and it broke out, in fact, a few years later.

In 1719 a Maltese pirate, flying the Spanish flag, captured an English ship, brought it to Valetta and sold it. The pirate's identity had been established and the usual development ensued. There was an English squadron in Naples under Admiral Sir George Byng. He decided to act at once, but with the utmost courtesy; in those days diplomats did not bang the table with their fists, let alone with their shoes, neither did admirals. Sir George sent the *Dreadnought* to Malta with Captain Saunders. One of the midshipmen was the Admiral's son, Pattee Byng, who kept a diary and wrote a lively account of what took place. When they arrived at Malta, Perellos was very old and at death's door; so Saunders and his staff were entertained by the Bailly von Königsegg and the Bailly de Langon 'who had been General of the Galleys and had distinguished himself most remarkably against the Turks', wrote Pattee Byng. The officers were entertained for several days by all the high dignitaries of the Order; they were shown round St John and the Armoury, taken round the fortifications, invited to a concert at Prince Vahini's palace and afterwards to a garden party at Verdalla. Young Byng asked many questions about the organization of the Order and the duties of the Knights. He summed up his impressions as follows:

'These Knights of Malta are in perpetual war with the Turks and think themselves obliged to attack them whenever they meet them, though much inferior in strength. They very much encourage one another in this spirit, and in their discourse are full of the achievements and valourous exploits of the Knights of their Order in former times, which they value themselves much upon; and which are carefully handed down to them by tradition and pleases their minds and inflames their spirits, and indeed they told us of so many extraordinary feats done in former times by the Knights of their Order, that one would imagine them so many Don Quixotes, and they referred us to their histories for the truth of many of this. This is the sort of spirit they busy one another up in, and it is not to be wondered at, when they shall do very extraordinary actions, since they who are the blood of the first families in Europe are nursed up in the notions of acquiring fame to themselves and their Order, and are wishing for all occasions of signalizing themselves against the enemies of Christ, and keep constantly cruising upon them with their men-of-war and galleys.'

Meanwhile, discussions were proceeding between Captain Saunders on the one side and the Chevaliers Sansidoni and de Montmorency-Laval, 'two of the ablest men of the Order', on the other. On October 27, 1719, an agreement was reached and a treaty signed, but the matter could not rest at that. The whole matter had to be settled once and for all and a solution reached, or at least an attempt should be made to reach one. It was realized by everyone that the situation was significant for both parties. An international conference was to take place in Cambrai in a few months' time: it would be advisable to have the Order's international situation settled there. To begin with, the Order should send an Envoy Extraordinary to London to discuss the whole problem with the Foreign Secretary. Saunders agreed to give any help within his power. It was decided that the Chevalier Joseph de Montmorency-Laval should go.

He was forty-seven and his family was one of the oldest in France. He had been received into the Order when he was thirteen and had begun his career by serving in the French navy under de Tourville, to whom he was distantly related. He was with him in June 1690, when his fleet sailed from Brest to Pevensey to fight the English and Dutch fleets, and the young man wrote a very good account of the battle.[5] Montmorency-Laval had fought extremely well; then, after some years in the French navy, he went to Malta to take up his knightly duties.

In 1715 he was appointed French Consul in Valetta, 'the King's Man', after his predecessor the Chevalier de Tincourt had left to be cut for stone in Italy; he survived the operation, which was unusual. The Consul was still one of the French Knights and his task was difficult and delicate, sometimes getting him into trouble with the Grand Master. A Malta colleague described him as 'a man of high birth, with a noble mind, no fortune, knowing all the customs and habits of foreign countries'.[6] Montmorency-Laval displayed great tact, an important virtue. He spent his time trying to soothe furious shipowners, angered by the outrages of the Maltese pirates.

Another of his problems was what to do when slaves (whether Christian or not) escaped from Turkish ships anchored in Malta. He succeeded in acquiring a wide and deep knowledge of legal problems connected with the sea. Turkish slaves had to be bought for the French galleys, and he was the one who dealt with that scandalous trade.

On December 12, 1719, he wrote to the French Regency Council to notify them that the Grand Master had appointed him Envoy Extraordinary to England: he was appointed in order to ask the Court of St James's for a settlement of the Order's status after the signing of a provisional agreement. Thus he had to request the Regent to grant him permission to fulfil these new duties: he would wait for his orders in Marseille.[7] The Regent permitted him to accept the appointment, as he was on the best possible terms with England.

Accordingly, Montmorency-Laval started out for England, having handed his consular duties over to the Chevalier de Montgontier. He left Valetta on January 18, 1720, a week after Perellos's death and the election of Zondadari. Three days later he was in Messina, having sailed on one of Langon's ships; the Court received him well, but he was disappointed to hear that Admiral Byng had just left for Palermo. He had been hoping to meet him.[8] On February 7th Montmorency arrived in Naples and met the Admiral, who had just arrived from Sicily. 'He received me with the greatest courtesy,' wrote the Chevalier, 'as a man who had not forgotten that I had had the honour to discuss the Order's interests with him.'[9] At the same time, Byng wrote to Cragg, the English Foreign Secretary:

'Upon my arrival at Naples I met here the Chevalier de Laval who acquainted me he is going to England (as I understand) in the quality of a minister from the Grand Master and Governor of Malta to supplicate the King's favour in relation to the prizes that have been carried into Malta. I take leave to acquaint you, Sir, he is a man of character and esteemed by the Religion of Malta and I am persuaded would deserve your attention to the address he shall make to you.'[10]

Laval spent a few days in Naples and met various friends;

he was eagerly collecting letters of introduction which might
be useful in England; at that time, a journey to England was
something of an adventure for a Knight of Malta. One letter
came from a very flamboyant character, Count Alexandre de
Bonneval, who, having been hounded out of the French service by the hatred and stupidity of one of Louis XIV's
ministers, was now serving the Emperor and was later to serve
the Turks and become a Moslem, assuming the name of Ahmet
Pasha. In Sicily, he was still fairly conventional, and his letter
to Cragg is charming:

'Sir, I am very glad to be able to take the opportunity of the
departure of the Commander de Montmorency-Laval to
remind Your Excellency that you have in this country a man
who respects and loves you with all his heart. We drank your
health and I charge you to drink mine when he is in London.
You won't be surprised by my concern for him when you
know that his own merit is very great and I am his near
relative; the Marquis de Bonneval [his elder brother] being the
Marquis de Laval's brother-in-law. He goes to your Court,
sent by the Grand Master of Malta, about some trouble which
has happened at sea. I trust that his negotiations are going to
be very successful if you are kind enough to grant him your
protection. I am sure that you will do so with as much pleasure
as I am Your Excellency's most humble and obedient servant.
Alexandre de Bonneval.'[11]

From Naples Laval proceeded to Rome, where he saw the
Pope. He was not unduly optimistic about the importance of
that call, but it had to be done, and he wrote to the new Grand
Master: 'the Pope is very pleasant: better make use of his
present good will', which was not to last.[12] Popes usually cold-
shouldered the Order's envoys; such a pleasant welcome was
therefore rather unexpected. Montmorency-Laval carefully
acquainted him with 'the violent state' of the Order.

His slow and solemn progress continued. In Florence he
saw old Cosimo III in the last stages of senile decay. In Genoa
he met the English envoy, d'Avenant, who wrote to London
at once, saying that his guest was 'a knight of distinguished
birth and recognized merit'.[13] On March 23rd Montmorency

was in Marseille and five days later in Paris, where he set to work with the Ambassador, the Bailly de Mesmes. He went to see the Regent and the Minister, Cardinal Dubois. Both gave him warm letters of introduction, and he also received one from John Law, the financier. The Regent wrote to the Prime Minister that 'he had a great affection for the Order of Malta, composed of the highest noblemen in Europe'.[14] Dubois added that he had been requested to provide a letter of introduction and he was responding to that request with pleasure.

Montmorency-Laval arrived in London on May 26th. He made contact with the French Ambassador, M. de Seneterre, at once and recorded:

'I begged him to take me to Lord Sunderland, Lord Stanhope and Mr Cragg. We did not find them at home, so we proceeded to St James's where we met Lord Stanhope, to whom I was presented by M. de Seneterre, and to whom I delivered the letters I had for him. The minister asked me whether I had seen the King: I said no, and that I was looking for the Master of Ceremonies to be taken to the Presence Chamber, so that he offered to present me to His Majesty. As I had some difficulty in agreeing, making him understand that I dreaded that Mr Cragg, to whose department I belonged, might be offended, he said that he would settle the matter with Mr Cragg. He then asked me in which function I wanted to be received; I answered, in no other than that of a Knight of Malta. So I entered the King's presence with the Minister, and I handed him the letters from His Royal Highness the Duke of Orleans, His Royal Highness of Tuscany and his Serene Highness the Grand Master.'

The presentation to George I was almost perfunctory and the Chevalier was slightly staggered by the lack of formality in the whole procedure. He wanted to hand the King his memoir, but the King told him at once that it had nothing to do with him and advised him to give it to Cragg. Such lack of interest was rather a shock to Montmorency.

After the Royal audience he was taken to Cragg, who was charming. He was also presented to the Prince and the Princess of Wales. Everyone was more than friendly towards

8. Bailly de Crussol, by Greuze

Portrait of a young Commander (unidentified) by Nattier

9. Matthew Prior (portrait attributed to A. Dahl, 1713)

Bailly Jacques de Chambray, by de Favray

Bailly de Mesmes (engraving by Caro fils after Raoulx)

Mgr de Saint-Simon, Bishop of Metz, by Rigaud

him and mildly surprised at the same time: it was the first time since the Reformation that an Envoy from Malta had been sent to the Court of St James.[15]

Nevertheless, the negotiations were protracted; in fact, they made no progress at all. Montmorency gave any number of reports, memoirs, printed letters and manuscript notes, yet things stagnated. However, on June 11th Cragg wrote to Montmorency:

'His Majesty commands me to let you know that he agrees that the Grand Master and the Order should have some authorized person to put forward their claim to the ministers of the States who are to meet in a conference at Cambrai. I can also tell you that, would the Grand Master entrust his interests to a person of your merit and distinction, His Majesty believes that nothing better could be done and you should be sent in that capacity to Cambrai.'[16]

It was extremely flattering, but Montmorency was getting restless. For one thing, there was a new war scare in Malta: the Turks were arming once more and France could do very little to help the Order, as her treasury was empty as usual. Montmorency discreetly suggested that English military help would be more than welcome, and he applied to Lord Polworth, sending him one more report.[17] On June 28th Montmorency left for Paris to prepare his documents and luggage for the Conference of Cambrai, which was shortly to open.

Before leaving England he wrote to Zondadari: 'Things have not ended to my entire satisfaction. Yet the King has been gracious enough to tell me that he would request his plenipotentiary to take up the Order's interests.'[18] But things went from bad to worse. Within a few days both Cragg and Lord Stanhope died suddenly and unexpectedly, for both were still young. Montmorency had to deal with Lord Carteret, the new Foreign Secretary, who knew nothing of the whole question, which had to be explained to him fully from the very beginning. The other person with whom Montmorency was in touch was Lord Polworth, who was as helpful as possible, but the innumerable papers the Chevalier had sent to the two dead Ministers were never found in their files and everything had to be rewritten. However, the letters of introduction were not lost: they are to be found in the Public Record Office. Montmorency remained in Cambrai until January 4, 1723. He had made a few points for the Order, though not all, but he was immensely pleased with his journey to England.

Shortly afterwards, provided with three commanderies (Louviers, Vaumont and Thou), he left Malta to assume in Paris the post of High Treasurer at the Grand Priory of France. He was eventually raised to the rank of Grand Cross and Bailly. In 1748 he succumbed to a stroke, having been a sick man for several years.

CHAPTER XI

ENGLISH KNIGHTS

❧❦❧

A FTER 1560, although it had not been suppressed, the Order was no longer recognized by England; but its properties had been confiscated. As a leading naval power in its own area, British sovereigns remained on courteous terms with the Grand Masters. Sir John Narbrough's Mediterranean cruises and his visits to Malta have already been mentioned. British fleets called at Valetta towards the end of the seventeenth century and a very special incident took place in 1687: the Duke of Grafton and Lord James Fitzjames visited the island. The Duke was twenty-four and his cousin seventeen. It is not known whether they were good friends: probably not. They were both illegitimate sons of kings and James II hated his nephews and had had the eldest executed. Yet, as the future Duke of Berwick was far more intelligent than his father, James possibly realized that his cousin was possessed of a pleasant personality, courage and enterprise.

In the summer of 1687 the two princes had gone to sea together. Grafton was in command of two ships, the *Hampshire* and the *Sedgemoor*. They were first entrusted with the duty of conveying the King of Portugal's fiancée, Princess Maria-Sophia of Neubourg, to Lisbon. The sea passage was a good one; nothing unexpected happened, the princess was safely delivered to Don Pedro II, and after a number of receptions at Court the two ships sailed south. On August 13th they passed a French fleet near Gibraltar, commanded by the Comte de Tourville, who by that time had left the Order of Malta. Salutes were duly exchanged.

Their first port of call was Algiers, where Grafton had to take the King's compliments to the Dey and redeem some Christian slaves. The young admiral was enthusiastically received, probably on account of his youth and good looks.

which he had inherited from his mother, the Duchess of Cleveland. He may have done some clever intelligence work in Algiers, for in the Public Record Office files is a list of the Algerian ships in 1687, which was certainly drawn up by Grafton or for him. The Dey's fleet consisted of nineteen vessels.[1] On October 6th Grafton was in Tunis; then he went to Tripoli and afterwards proceeded north, calling at Malta.

Fleming mentioned the visit of 'the Duke of Grafton, the King of England's natural son, and Lord Fitzjames, who is in the Order'.[2] This fact is not mentioned in his various biographies. It is possible that James II, rather doubtful as to what he could do for his numerous illegitimate children, was trying to get one or two into safe niches in the Order of Malta; he later got his second son by Arabella Churchill into the Order. Both were excused from their vows and both of them married.

On December 15, 1687, Grand Master Caraffa wrote to James II, telling him of his son's and his nephew's visit. They had been received as his representatives and Caraffa was careful to mention the fact that due honour had been paid to the Royal flag and that both young men had attracted much admiration.[3] The Grand Master took the visit as a proof of the King's respect for his religion and for the Order. He possibly did not know that Grafton was a Protestant. Anyhow, the princes were feasted all over the island. The Grand Master entertained them at his palace and treated them to a sung high mass at St John. There was a garden party at Verdalla, the Grand Masters' summer palace, surrounded by a small pine wood and an orange grove. They were shown the fortresses and the ships of the Order.

The Chevalier de Bataille, of the Langue de France, wrote to the Earl of Sunderland on December 9th, sending him a report of the visit, which has been lost. He added:

'It has pleased My Lord, Prince Fitzjames, to order me to let Your Grace know of his arrival in the island, his departure and all that happened while he was here with the Admiral Mylord the Duke of Grafton. I obey the order of a Prince who has such power over me and I trust that Your Grace will not be offended by the enclosed narrative, written to inform His Majesty of all that took place, if you think fit to show it. The short time the Princes spent here prevented them from writing to Your Grace, and they hope to be able to do so from Leghorn.'[4]

It is likely that Bataille was discreetly spying on the two young men. When they left, the Council of the Order decided to present Harry Fitzjames with a diamond heart which was entrusted to his elder brother.[5]

Grafton's fleet was back in England by the spring of 1688 and the cousins' careers were soon to part, as they took opposite sides when William of Orange landed in England. After 1688 a number of British noblemen applied for permission to join the Order of Malta. There had been none during the seventeenth century, possibly because they could find employment in the army and navy at home. When Jacobite refugees drifted to France, some of them in dire poverty, they realized that a Maltese knighthood might solve their financial problems. It scarcely ever did and their situation was always precarious. Technically, the Order only accepted noblemen belonging to one of the Langues through which they might be provided with a Commandery. There was no Langue d'Angleterre and no longer English or Scottish commanderies; consequently the Order was always very doubtful as to what to do with English or Scottish candidates. In the middle of the eighteenth century, Grand Master Vilhena wrote to a young Irishman who wanted to come to Malta that he should either obtain a Papal bull or a formal application from the Bailly d'Orleans, Grand Prior of France and the Regent's illegitimate son. The latter was the better choice.

Most of the Irish candidates were entered into the Langue de France. They usually applied to the Grand Master through one of the Stuart princes. James II had the Duke of Berwick made Grand Prior of England in 1689 at the time when, as he wrote to the Grand Master, 'he was leading a pretty rough and dangerous campaign against our rebellious subjects, who are at the same time the enemies of our religion'.[6] When James had withdrawn to St Germain, he often wrote to the Grand Master to forward applications from Irish refugees. After his death, the Old Pretender and his wife Clementina Sobieska almost specialized on that sort of correspondence. From Rome they sent many letters to the Grand Masters, who always replied in the most courteous way and often granted them the favours they asked, more than most Continental princes cared to do. There was no correspondence with Prince Charles-Edward, but a certain amount with the Cardinal of York, who seems to have known Rohan personally.

There were two main problems. One was purely financial: how to avoid paying 'rights of passage', the heavy entrance fees into the Order. Time and time again the Old Pretender and his wife wrote on behalf of some young Irishman—Dillon, Macdonnell, Geraldin or Barnwal—begging for time to pay or for complete exemption from payment, and they often carried their point. The Grand Masters often tried to please the Stuarts, though they were not over-optimistic about their possible restoration; but the Order gave no help at all in 1715 or 1745 and maintained friendly relations with the Hanover dynasty.

In 1718 a young Macdonnell made things very difficult for the Pretender, who had given him an introduction to Perellos. He was an impetuous, unreliable young man, who in Malta promptly quarrelled with everybody and ran away. Perellos was furious and James Stuart wrote many letters of apology.[7]

This unhappy episode did not cause him to abandon his interest in candidates for knighthood. By 1723 he was again writing to Grand Master Vilhena to press the application of Nicholas Geraldin, who had been accepted by the Order ten years earlier when he was a little boy and was now 'a wise, prudent youth'. This most eligible young man was highly regarded by the Pretender, who granted all the favours he asked for, recommending him to Vilhena warmly and arranging for him to take his vows, not in Valetta, but in Rome in the Pretender's private chapel in his palace on the Piazza di Santi Apostoli. Finally, Geraldin was received into the Langue de France and eventually granted a French commandery and a Grand Cross.[8]

In 1731 the Pretender made another request: he wanted the Grand Priory of England, a completely empty title, for Pedro Bonaventure Fitzjames, a brother of the third Duke of Berwick. The Grand Master complied, but young Fitzjames, like his grandfather and great-uncle, remained in the Order for only a couple of years, being then released from his vows in order to marry.

The Pretender helped the Dillon family for years. The first Dillon had followed James II to St Germain. His son Arthur had raised a regiment in the King of France's service and married Christina, daughter of Ralph Sheldon, James II's equerry. They had ten children and very little money. Three of the children entered the Church and when the third son, James Dennis, wished to go to Malta there was an endless correspondence between the Pretender, his wife and the Grand Master to allow him free admission. The Grand Master could not very well refuse, and when James Dennis was sixteen he was allowed to go to Valetta without paying his entrance fee.

The Pretender sometimes helped French subjects. In 1746, he recommended the Chevalier de Breteuil to Pinto because 'his mother was one of my subjects';[9] Mme le Tonnelier de Breteuil was Laura O'Brien of Clare; she was born in St Germain in 1697 and had been christened in the castle chapel in which she was married in 1720. The Chevalier de Breteuil was her second son and he made a fine career in the Order, ending as Ambassador to Paris in 1785.

There were a few surprising episodes. In 1778 Louis Edward Drummond of Melfort sent in his proofs of nobility in order to enter the Langue de France: he was in a very strange position. It seems that he was a French subject and on his father's side was descended from one of the oldest families of Scotland, dating back to 1060, though on his mother's side the line was much weaker. She was a Mlle de la Porte, probably rich but of very recent nobility. Count Drummond of Melfort had certainly 'gilded his coat of arms' when marrying her. His son's proofs were not accepted, a situation that was fairly frequent, though such difficulties were often overlooked. The matter was argued for several years. The young man had been born in Edinburgh in 1767 and was establishing his proofs through the Lyon King of Arms. He was connected with all the great families in Scotland, including the Stuarts, since he was a descendant of James II of Scotland. Yet the heraldry experts of the Langue de France insisted on the lack of quarters on his mother's side. Eventually Drummond was angered and applied to a higher authority, getting a papal brief to the effect that his proofs 'were good and valid'. That document had to be accepted, and on January 3, 1785, after a struggle which had lasted for seven years, Drummond of Melfort was allowed to make his first caravan: he was eighteen.[10]

The strangest episode concerning English subjects and the Order of Malta took place in 1783. On June 3rd, Viscount Torrington wrote from Brussels to the Duke of Manchester, Secretary of State, to put to him the case of Dennis O'Sullivan, who had been turned down by the Order of Malta. Though living in Brussels, he was an English subject and it was unthinkable that such an insult should be offered to an Englishman merely because the Order had already far too many Irish members—since this appears to have been the reason for rejecting his proofs of nobility. The young man's family was old and of unquestionable nobility.

The Duke of Manchester agreed to help and wrote to the Queen of France to seek her assistance. He also wrote personally to Grand Master de Rohan, who answered through his Ambassador in Paris, the Bailly d'Argenteuil, successor to Breteuil. The answer was typical of Rohan. In a clear, straightforward fashion he told Manchester that the difficulty arose from the fact that there were no English commanderies; technically, therefore, the statutes of the Order barred English candidates. But the Grand Master could always try and make things easier, and so did Rohan. His courtesy and eager desire to please were well known and he displayed them once more. Above all else, he hated hurting people's feelings and in this case he found a clever though intricate solution. He would accept O'Sullivan into the Langue de France, while allowing him to make his proofs in the English fashion, through the College of Heralds.[11]

The Order's attitude towards English candidates was a good example of the Grand Master's excellent manners, permitting a satisfactory solution of the Order's intricate regulations.

CHAPTER XII

THE CHEVALIER D'AYDIE
AND MLLE AÏSSÉ

᎒᎒᎒

LOUIS XIV was dead, the new King was five years old
and the Regent, his uncle, the Duke of Orleans, was an
intelligent, brave and good-looking man of forty-one
who had been kept in complete idleness by the old King.
Being naturally lazy, voluptuous and very rich, sickened by
the narrow bigotry of the Court, bored by an unattractive
wife (one of Louis XIV's illegitimate daughters) there was but
one thing for him to do: amuse himself. He did this very well.
When on the King's death he assumed the Regency, in very
difficult conditions, he went on amusing himself, though he
worked as hard as he could at the same time. But at such a
pace he could not live very long.

One of his daughters had married her cousin, the Duke de
Berry, Louis XIV's grandson, a worthy, dull young man who
adored her and whose love she rewarded very badly. When he
died of a hunting accident at twenty-two, the young dowager
duchess kept her own court (to which she was entitled because
she was a Princess of the Blood) and she soon became the talk
of the town. Saint-Simon, who was her father's intimate friend,
wrote of her: 'She was prodigy of wit, pride, ingratitude and
madness, and also of lust and stubbornness.' A thoroughly unbearable person who was idolized by her father to such a point
that the idea was mooted that they were incestuous lovers.
After many other amorous adventures, she discovered a very
unlikely favourite and fell madly in love with him. His name
was Sicard-Armand de Rions and, quoting Saint-Simon again,
was 'a fat boy with pale, heavy cheeks covered with pimples,
looking very much like a large abscess'. The Regent's mother,
the fierce old Palatine Princess, called him The Toad. Eventually, the Duchess married him secretly. She died of overeating

and a miscarriage when she was barely twenty-five.

The Toad was descended from an old Périgord family and had brought with him a young cousin, Blaise-Marie d'Aydie, whom he introduced to his duchess. D'Aydie was born in the Chateau de Vaugoubert, in Périgord, in 1692 and, in contrast to his cousin, was good-looking in a charming, witty way. He was the youngest son of a large family and so was created a Knight of Malta in 1713, when he was twenty-one, and he probably went to Malta at once. He made his caravans and behaved well, being much interested in everything connected with the sea, but he did not take his vows. He never took them: he could not bear the thought of losing an inch of his liberty.

On leaving Malta he went to Court and Rions took him into the most intimate circle of the little court the Duchess de Berry held at the Luxembourg. D'Aydie was the Duchess's lover for some time and Rions did not think fit to assume the position of jealous rival. D'Aydie was also a member of the groups which met at the Palais Royal, invited by the Regent, or at the Temple, where his host was the Bailly de Vendôme, Grand Prior of France. It was a suitable haunt for a young Knight of Malta, the only trouble being that Vendôme, an illegitimate grandson of Henri IV, was one of the outstanding rakes of the time. He was a witty, cultured, good-looking man and his friends were among the wittiest men of France; they included Chaulieu, La Fare, Anthony Hamilton, Alexandre de Bonneval and the very young Voltaire. D'Aydie probably met there the man who was to be his life-long friend, the Chevalier de Froullay, eight years older than himself, a delightful person, both pious and broad-minded, fitting everywhere, and being ready always to help or advise in an intelligent way.

By 1720 d'Aydie was one of the most popular young men in Paris. He was 'full of wit and of spirit, a Gaul brought up in Athens with the loyalty of the former and the charm of the Athenian', according to Mme de Créqui, Froullay's niece, who knew him well. And then, in some fashionable drawing-room, he met Mlle Aïssé.

Aïssé is one of the appealing and surprising women of the eighteenth century, who still retain their mystery and add much grace to history. The broad lines of her story are well known.

The Marquess Charles de Ferriol, French Ambassador to Constantinople, had adopted many Turkish habits during the many years he lived there. He used to buy lovely slaves and live with them Turkish fashion; when he returned to France on leave he either freed them or took them with him, marrying them off after providing them with handsome dowries. Three of them are known: two of them married well, the third and youngest was Aïssé.*

She was born in Circassia, 'in the Kingdom of Cabarca', according to a French legal document,[1] and she had been kidnapped when she was scarcely more than a baby. The man who sold her in the slave market of Constantinople said that she was a princess: it may or may not have been true. Ferriol bought her when she was about four and took her back to France in 1698. As his own Christian name was Charles, he had her christened in Lyons with the names Charlotte-Elisabeth; they were on their way to Paris. She always retained her native name of Haydee, slightly altered into Aïssé. In Paris the Ambassador entrusted her to his sister-in-law, Mme de Ferriol, who placed her in a convent.

She was given an excellent education and very little real schooling. For instance, her spelling was always more than erratic. When she went back to her protectress, she was brought up with the latter's two sons, the young Counts of Argental and Pont-de-Veyle, who loved her as a slightly older sister and were always devoted to her. She was at daggers drawn with Mme de Ferriol's sister, Mme de Tencin, a beautiful, depraved woman who was under some semi-religious vows. Incidentally, when Ferriol sailed back to Turkey in 1699, his ship had called at Malta and he had made things very difficult, stating that as he was the King's representative he should always sit at the Grand Master's right. The Grand

---

* I have made a special study of the best-known documents about Aïssé, especially her *Letters*, published by Rieu in 1787, and have come to the conclusion that they are spurious. I cannot repeat here this long and intricate affair and I refer the reader to two articles I published in the *Revue des Deux Mondes* (1954 and 1962); also to my edition of Prévost's *Histoire d'une Grecque Moderne*. The only letters I quote here are those of undoubted authenticity, as their MSS are known: two are kept by Aïssé's descendants, the Bonnevals, and three are in the Bibliotheque Publique et Universitaire in Geneva.

Master refused and, after heated arguments, they agreed not to meet, Perellos merely sending presents, drinks, ice-cream and a huge sword-fish, and allowing Ferriol to drive in his own magisterial coach. On the other hand, in order to be unpleasant to the Grand Master, the Grand Inquisitor received Ferriol in the most obsequious fashion.[2]

Aïssé had entered a very fashionable, cultured and depraved society. The ladies who were supposed to look after her suggested she should become the Regent's mistress, but she refused. Yet she was not always adamant. 'She was young, beautiful, sentimental and idle,' wrote Mme de Crequy, who knew her well. It seems that her first admirers were members of the English Embassy in Paris, men of great charm and elegance who were extremely popular at Court. Among them was Bolingbroke, who flirted pleasantly with his 'dear Circassian', his 'lovely Aïssé', as he calls her in his letters. He was to become her devoted friend, on whom she could always rely. At that time he was living with Mme de Vilettes, whom he was to marry later, and she was Aïssé's friend as well. Matthew Prior flirted with her, too, but his mistress was Mme de Tencin, and it was in her house that he may have met Aïssé. He called her his 'Fair Infidel'. It is obvious that, though she was a good Christian, she was making the most of her exotic origin.

Another man made a deeper impression upon her affections: he was Charles Mordaunt, Earl of Peterborough, who was fifty-six at the time. He had been sent on a mission to France and had been extremely well received by the King and his minister Torcy. When he left, Prior wrote to him: 'As to your private comments, the Christian as well as the Mahometan are your servants, upon which condition the Mahometan will, I presume, resign her body for her soul. You know, as she is a slave, it is not at her disposal.' Knowing Prior's often insolent, pithy style, it is easy to draw a conclusion.[3]

By that time Ferriol was back in Paris. He was old and broken in health; his last diplomatic mission had been a failure. He found that Aïssé had grown into a beautiful young woman; he claimed his rights and made her his mistress. He had always loved her from afar, first as a little girl to whom he had sent scarves and jewels, then in a more ambiguous way; he explained the whole situation to her in an undated letter. It is repulsive, yet the man's love is obvious:

'When I rescued you from the hands of the Infidel and bought you, I did not intend to make myself miserable for years to come. . . . My intention was to make you some day either my daughter or my mistress. The same fate has decreed that you shall be both, as I cannot separate love from affection and inflamed desires from a father's tenderness.'

He wanted her to be absolute mistress of all his possessions and he had already endowed her very generously. There is some possibility that this letter, the style of which is rather stilted, very literary, and quite different from Ferriol's straightforward, simple dispatches, may be spurious. The manuscript no longer exists. He was either not jealous or he was very blind, as he never seemed to suspect the fact that Aïssé, though she was kind and affectionate, loved elsewhere.

It was some time in 1719 that she met d'Aydie and it was love at first sight for both of them, but of different kinds. For the young woman it was a devouring passion which engulfed her life. For the man it was at first a flattering experience, for Aïssé was a renowned beauty and with her romantic Eastern past a picturesque creature. He then settled into his love with pleasure, giving her a constant, quiet, sincere, even devoted love, basking in her adoration, putting up with her fits of temper and remaining faithful to her until her death. By 1720, and probably earlier, they were lovers.

In 1720 Bolingbroke was back in France, out of power and exiled. He and his mistress, Mme de Vilettes, whom he was to marry soon afterwards, knew d'Aydie and helped the two lovers to come together. So did Mme de Ferriol's sons. One of the few extant letters from Aïssé to d'Aydie seems to have been written in 1720. She implored him to come to her as soon as possible, the next morning at the latest. She had something urgent to tell him: 'It is not very important, but I cannot wait longer to tell you,'[4] and she explains how he can call on her without attracting Ferriol's attention. The Ambassador's suspicion, if he had any, was of no importance, as d'Aydie's presence in the house could easily be explained. Most likely, what she had to tell him was that she was with child. By the end of the year the Bolingbrokes invited her to stay at their country house, La Source, Bolingbroke wrote: 'Mlle Aïssé is coming and she gives up the pleasures of Paris for some time. She is perhaps right to visit her friends at the back of beyond in their province; others go and call on their mothers.' On another occasion Bolingbroke wrote that he was expecting her: 'The Turk is her excuse and the real reason a certain Christian whom I knew well.'[5]

Their child, a girl, was born in April 1721; she was christened Célénie. Mme de Vilettes looked after the mother and took the baby to England to be brought up. In 1722 Ferriol died, bequeathing his fortune to Aïssé. The young woman, with great dignity, refused it and gave it back to his family. His death did not change her life very much: she stayed with Mme de Ferriol and saw d'Aydie openly. She had met all his friends, including Froullay, who liked and admired her and sent her affectionate messages when he returned to Malta to take up a command in the Order's navy. D'Aydie had to divide his time between Périgord, where he looked after his estate, and Paris: he had a rank in the army and at Court. In 1723, leaving for Périgord for one month, he wanted to avoid a heart-breaking parting with Aïssé, and he did not say goodbye. She sent him a frantic, beautiful letter, full of love and violence:

'I can see you rely more on the violence of my love than on the strength of my reason. I believe that to please you, I should reveal nothing but the latter. The most bitter, exquisite, maddest pain grips and still grips me in a terrible way. No one has been so near madness as I. You are lucky, not knowing how terrible and eager love can be.'[6]

Her letter rambles on and on, penned at top speed. D'Aydie was promptly forgiven, of course.

A later journey was longer. In 1724 he went to Poland, where a French army was fighting, and he came back, having been nicknamed the Sarmatian. While he was away Aïssé had been to England with Lady Bolingbroke—she was married by that time. Her husband wrote to Mme de Ferriol: 'Have you news of Aïssé? Lady Bolingbroke wrote from Dover: she arrived on Friday after the best crossing in the world. She was hardly troubled by sea-sickness but her companion gave back her dinner to the fishes.' Lady Bolingbroke was calling on her husband's former political friends and associates, to try and get permission for him to return to England, which was granted. Meanwhile, Aïssé collected her little daughter, whom she brought back to France and put into a convent in Sens. Then, when d'Aydie went away, she could see her and stay with her for a few days.

A little later, d'Aydie offered to marry her: he was perfectly sincere, though possibly not very eager, as he hated any tie which might hinder his beloved liberty. Aïssé refused him, writing to the Chevalier de Froullay, who seems to have been one of her advisers: 'I am too great a friend of his to marry him.'[7] It was not, as has been suggested, in order not to bar him from promotion in Malta: this was not possible, anyway, since he was not a professing Knight. It was out of respect for him: though nobody ever seems to have minded, she knew she had a somewhat heavy past: the slave market (though she was only a baby at the time), the Old Turk, Lord Peterborough. From dignity and tact she turned down his offer. She was thirty-four, middle-aged for an Eastern woman, and she already felt the first pangs of the sickness that was to kill her, tuberculosis. Her refusal did not change her life in the least. D'Aydie saw her every day when he was in Paris, loving her in a calm, pleasant, steady way, feeling perfectly happy with her, and once, when she was visiting her little daughter in Sens, he sent her a delightful letter, ending: 'We both obey our hearts. My paper overflows and I have not yet repeated that I love you.'

There is a story that she was compelled by her Genevese friend, Mme Calandrini, to renounce her love and to part from her lover. The whole episode seems to be a well-written, though completely fanciful piece of fiction, written long after Aïssé's death, cleverly worked out in a number of spurious letters which were only published in 1787. She did not know Mme Calandrini very intimately, and the one letter to her which has been preserved in a contemporary copy is very different from the printed text; the other letters do not make sense from an historical point of view, and after 1780 the fashion was to write tearful novels about unhappy love stories, like *Clarissa Harlowe*, *La nouvelle Héloise*, and Mme de Tencin's *Malheurs de l'amour*.

Mlle Aïssé stayed with the Ferriols, going with them to their estate in Bresse, and staying also with Genevese friends she had met in Paris, several members of the Tronchin family, and Mme Calandrini, whose descendants altered or forged what emerged as her *Lettres*. She attended Lady Bolingbroke devotedly during her illness in Reims. It seems also that she sometimes went to Périgord with d'Aydie, staying with him at his Chateau de Mayac.[8] Gradually her condition became worse. By the end of 1732 she was dying and d'Aydie never left her. Her last request to him seems to have been for a less ardent, more brotherly love: she could not bear more. He replied in writing, to avoid a heart-breaking scene, complying with her wish. Yet it is possible that this letter is spurious too, as well as Aïssé's, for both are known only through the published *Lettres*, which are completely unreliable. Anyhow, the letter, if true, was written six weeks at most before her death. What is certain is that d'Aydie never left her and she breathed her last in his arms in March 1733.

D'Aydie was completely shattered by her death, but he shouldered at once the duty he owed to her beloved memory: he looked after their daughter, Célénie, bringing her up, not as an illegitimate daughter, but as the only child of an adored mother. One of the Ferriol brothers was her official guardian; as he was one of d'Aydie's best friends, he had the Chevalier appointed instead. Célénie remained in Sens for several years: she was about twelve when her mother died and was well looked after. As for d'Aydie, he left Paris. In 1733 he had been appointed lieutenant in a company of Gardes Françaises in the Gardes du Corps and he was sent to Germany, where France was now fighting. On August 5, 1734, he wrote d'Argental, his daughter's guardian, from Oppenheim. He asked for news of the child, as he was sorry to hear that her temper was so bad. Could d'Argental make sure that her teeth were carefully looked after? He went on: 'We are pressing towards Mainz without any thought but to carry on—*fruges consumere nati* —such is the vocation of the largest, and possibly the most illustrious, part of our army. We badly need some initiative from Prince Eugene of Savoy to compel us to win a victory, as Mercy did some time ago.'[9]

When d'Aydie returned to France, his romantic life and his brilliant military record made him very popular. Voltaire, who knew him well, told everyone that he had drawn his portrait as a Knight 'without fear and without reproach', as did Coucy in his last tragedy, *Adelaide du Guesclin*. Let us hope that this is not a very lifelike portrait for Coucy was a bore and *Adelaide* one of his worst and completely unsuccessful tragedies. The Chevalier de Froullay was back in France; he had been promoted Bailly and the two friends often met. Did they mention Aïssé? Though her name never occurs in the letters which passed between them after her death, it is very likely, as Froullay had been one of her great friends. D'Aydie supervised his daughter's education carefully and the girl was becoming strikingly beautiful and her temper losing its asperity.

A few years later, in 1740, d'Aydie retired from the army and went to live in his castle of Mayac. Célénie was nineteen and he took her with him. Their home-coming was something like a triumphal ride. All the young noblemen of the surrounding chateaux came to meet them and rode beside their coach. Three months later Célénie married one of them, Pierre de Jaubert, Viscount de Nanthia, an intelligent young man who was in love with her and remained so. His family was of great nobility though impecunious, but she had a large dowry.

Then d'Aydie settled down in his chateau, calling on the young couple, on brothers and sisters scattered throughout the vicinity and on numerous friends. He hunted energetically, despite the asthma and gout to which he had always been prey. He sometimes went to Paris and called on the Bailly de Froullay, who was now the Order's Ambassador to Versailles. D'Aydie kept in touch with the Order, though he admitted he was but 'a *cavaliere d'albergo*, he who has never taken his vows and would not dream of doing so' (to quote a letter to Froullay).[10] He gave a lively description of the quarrel and reconciliation between the Grand Prior of Orleans and Bailly de Conflans, who had violently abused each other at a meeting of the council. The Bailly's nephew fought a duel with Orleans and was badly wounded, after which they forgave each other. Froullay was terribly active in Paris, discharging his duties and attending court, and d'Aydie admired him from afar, feeling happy and lazy in his rural peace and quiet. He tried to suggest to Froullay that he was overworking and when, in 1752, Froullay was sent on a difficult mission to Frederick II, the Bailly suggested he would be delighted to take his friend with him, d'Aydie backed out at once. Of course, if Froullay could not do without him, he would go but he would rather not! Froullay tried hard to interest him in religion, but d'Aydie politely refused to follow his lead: 'I'm afraid the devil whispers in my ear that devout persons are not always like you. Otherwise I would do so, to become just like you,' he wrote.

In the Mediterranean, the constant friction between Naples and Malta was coming very near to war, and in 1763 Naples stopped all ships going to Malta, and Neapolitans, in consequence, started a lively and flourishing smuggling trade. Grand Master Pinto summoned all the Knights to Malta. This was the call to general mobilization to which one had to resort when danger was increasing. D'Aydie took the matter to heart. He wrote to Froullay:

'I am old and gouty, the Religion never gave me, nor did I ever ask for, anything, but I am most attached to it, and were things to come to such a pitch that it would require the help of her children, you can be certain that I would not wait one minute to leave for Malta. Labour, money, our own lives, all we have is at the Order's disposal.'[11]

He meant it. And he mentioned another old Knight, Riberac, almost as old and gouty as himself, and much poorer, who would 'sell his shirt and go'. By that time, the French Court had taken the matter in hand and used such forcible arguments that Naples was compelled to stop threatening the Grand Master. D'Aydie was sixty-two by that time, a ripe old age in the eighteenth century.

His conscience was at rest and he continued to lead a healthy and quiet life. There is no proof that he had any other mistress after Aïssé's death—certainly no liaison of any long standing.

He had remained in contact with former Paris friends, Mme du Deffand, President Henault and the two Ferriol brothers. His tender, delicate letters to his daughter after her wedding enable the reader to believe that he faithfully remembered the lovely Circassian even unto death. When Mme de Nanthia's daughter was born, he gave Célénie her mother's portrait, writing in a most charming way about the woman who, whatever his former career may have been, remained his one great love. As for his daughter, he idolized her. 'My dear daughter, I shall arrive at your castle at four. I would be delighted to find a fire in the parlour and your little nose at the gate,' he once wrote.[12]

He used to visit her often, being still robust and lively when he was not tortured by gout; he roamed in the fields with his gun and his dog. One day he caught cold; congestion of the lungs developed and he never left his bed again. He quickly realized that his end was near and he met it calmly. He summed up his life and felt he had been lucky, said goodbye to the Nanthias, their child, his brother and sister, who had been summoned in haste, and 'spent his last hours in a world of remembrance', wrote Célénie, thinking of Aïssé. Death came on January 14, 1761.

CHAPTER XIII

BAILLY SAGRAMOSO'S GRAND TOUR

❧❀❧

ONE of the greatest assets of the Order was that its members usually succeeded, almost without training, in becoming administrators, diplomats, economists and almost anything, even though their education—when they had received any—was only intended to make them into sailors or soldiers. The eighteenth century knew nothing of specialization. Men who had plenty of common sense, and sometimes unconventional ideas, improvised and often did well. The Order was not weighted down by bureaucracy and red tape; in fact, it had rather too little, but it left its members' hands and minds free. One of its brilliant unspecialized diplomats was Bailly Michele Sagramoso.

He was born in Verona in 1720, the son of Orazio Sagramoso, Palatine Count. He studied at the University of Bologna, leading the gay life of any rich young man, and he acquired a wide, if slightly erratic culture. The sudden death of his young mistress shattered this pleasant life for a time, and in the depths of despair he retired into a cloister. After a short while he realized that he was not meant for a contemplative sheltered life and he came out again into the world, but he sent his proofs of nobility to Valetta in order to join the Order of Malta.[1] There was no difficulty about his admission. In 1741, on a legal deed signed in Verona by his father, he is mentioned as 'on his caravans in the service of the Order of Malta'. He then took the habit and possibly realized that the Order was providing him with the means to obey a new passion, that of travelling. Either in or out of the service of the Order, he could travel far and wide. There were those who said that, at the same time, he peddled his father's wine.[2]

Travelling in the eighteenth century meant meeting important people everywhere, and Sagramoso had a gift for making friends. He was much more cultured than most Knights. His French was perfect, he had read the French philosophers, Condillac and Malebranche among others; he was interested in geology and botany, in philology, in physics, and he loved meeting people, whom he kept entranced with his witty, lively conversation. He was good-looking, a pleasant companion and a great favourite with the ladies. He was also able to evince more manly virtues when necessary. This very gifted young man was going to prove himself an ideal diplomat.

When he had done with his caravans, he was given his first real opportunity to travel. The French Ambassador to Constantinople, M. de Castellane, asked Sagramoso to accompany him to Turkey. At the Embassy, Sagramoso may have met the Comte de Bonneval in the last stages of his fantastic career, who by that time was Ahmet Pasha, Commander of the Artillery and one of the secret advisers of the French Ambassador.[3] After a while, Sagramoso went back to Malta, was made a captain of the galleys and served at sea for five years.

When his command was over, he left the island and decided to travel again. He began with Genoa, where he met Maffei, then he went to Germany. This Italian was mostly attracted by northern countries. He visited Hamburg, Lubeck and Berlin, then went over to Denmark and then Sweden. There he saw most libraries and private collections. He met Tessin, the ex-Ambassador to France and an outstanding collector, and he was introduced to Linnaeus, the botanist. Either with him, or with his advice, he made several botanical expeditions, extending as far as Lapland.

In Stockholm he met Wargentin, the Swedish astronomer, whom he put in touch with several Italian scholars, a French naturalist, Seguier, and a Swiss astronomer, de Rivaz, who had devised a new telescope. Because Wargentin wanted to correspond with Loys de Cheseaux, a brilliant young mathematician, Sagramoso, when in Switzerland, brought him the Swedish scholar's letter and suggested sending him notes about a solar eclipse which was about to take place; but the young man died a few months later.[4]

He also met Dr Johann Ihre, a leading philologist, with whom he discussed the origins of languages, and what Leibnitz and Sparvenfeldt had written on the subject. Sagramoso's letter to Ihre[5] displays a slightly superficial, but intensely sincere love of learning. He offered to get books for Ihre, and asked for duplicates of Leibnitz's letters about some philological subjects. Somehow, Sagramoso met Count Henning Gyllenborg, possibly at court, where he was presented to the King. Gyllenborg was a scholar, and so were several members of his family.[6] Thanks to Gyllenborg, probably, Sagramoso was received into the Academy of Sweden on April 16, 1748. In his speech, subsequently published, he mentioned his studies of magnets, compasses and some points of meteorology. I have failed to find whether he published anything on such very varied subjects: his articles, if any, may be lost in some obscure scholarly magazine. He must have been one of the very few, and certainly the first, Knights of Malta to be paid such an honour.

With the coming of the summer, after his Lapland trip, he went to Russia, arriving at the time of Princess Sophia of Anhalt-Zerbst's wedding to the heir of the throne, the Czarevitch Peter. He met the young couple and also the Empress Elizabeth, who liked him very much. He also made friends with the Princess's brother, the young Prince of Anhalt. He was handed over to Count Razoumowsky, the President of the Imperial Academy, brother of the Empress's lover and father of that Count Razoumowsky to whom Beethoven later inscribed several quartets. Razoumowsky showed him round the Academy and Sagramoso realized that everything in that large, mysterious and threatening country deserved thorough study. Then he went back to Germany and into Switzerland.

Again he met all the people worth meeting: Bernouilli in Basle, Haller in Berne. He described the latter as a 'Sybarite in a Spartan country'. His next stop was Geneva, and both the city and the lake delighted him. It seems that during most of the time the weather was bad and he was treated to one of the unpleasant aspects of the lake, with huge waterspouts rising between the raging waves and the clouds. There had been similar storms a few years earlier and Sagramoso was shown what had been written about them. Later the weather cleared and he liked the lake so much that he regretted he could not settle on its banks and live in pure and rural happiness. Admiration for that lovely landscape was expressed by many travellers before Jean-Jacques Rousseau made it almost compulsory. There were other striking landscapes in the neighbourhood of the city. Sagramoso ascended the Salève and collected fossilized shells; then, pushing further inland, he went to Chamonix. By that time—1749 or 1750—the valley itself was well known, yet it was still a difficult journey with just one bad inn at the end. Sagramoso did not halt in the valley or even at the Montenvers: according to his biographer, Bertolla, he visited 'a meadow completely surrounded with ice'. Could this have been the Jardin de Talèfre? If so, it was a very daring expedition, for the place was visited only by crystal seekers and chamois hunters. Sagramoso did in fact collect some crystals during his expedition.

Back in Geneva, he was shown round the library by Gabriel Cramer, a charming man of great culture and a leading scientist, and he met Councillor Dupan.[7] During his stay in Switzerland he wrote to his Swedish friend, Count Gyllenborg, offering to put him in touch with Swiss scholars who could provide him with news of what was happening 'in their climate'. He tried to enlist the help of Laurent Garcin in Neuchâtel and Charles Bonnet in Geneva, a rather pompous, kind man who was interested mostly in polyps and bees. He also sent Gyllenborg a list of books which would interest him, explaining how they could be posted to Sweden. He studied the history of Switzerland and collected books on the subject.[8] He completed his Swiss tour by a visit to Zurich and Schaffhausen.

Then he proceeded to Holland. Among other people, he met two colleagues from Malta who had come to order ships for the Grand Master, the Chevaliers d'Aynac and de Charmail: they had lost their credentials and were at their wits' end. As usual, Sagramoso knew everybody and helped them at court. He put them in touch with the right person and by the time they left everything had been smoothed out and they were presented with gold snuff-boxes by the Stadthouder.

Back he went to Osnabruck and Hamburg, afterwards crossing to England. He was presented to King George II and the Prince of Wales at Windsor. He went to Oxford and was enthusiastic about the Bodleian library. England was one of the countries which delighted him most. In 1751 he was in

France and spent a whole year travelling up and down the kingdom. One of the men he knew best was the naturalist Duhamel de Monceau. He was acquainted with Montesquieu and discussed his works with him. He was also acquainted with Malesherbes who invited him to his chateau. Finally, he returned to Italy in 1753 and was appointed the Order's Ambassador to Venice in the following year.

The city agreed with him. He met many curious people, one of whom was Lady Mary Wortley Montague. They met at a concert in 1757 and he whispered to her that when in London he had had the pleasure of hearing her daughter, Lady Bute, singing. Lady Mary was unpleasant as usual, and in a letter complained bitterly of his misplaced courtesy: he talked much too loudly![10] Mme du Boccage was a much more pleasant guest: she was a third-rate French poetess, but an intelligent and much-travelled woman who kept a vivid memory of her trips in gondolas with Sagramoso. The Ambassador was elected a member of Gozzi and Goldoni's Academies and was one of the most popular figures in the city. He wrote to Wargentin: 'Having travelled all round Europe, I have at last come to rest among the Venetian lagoons; moreover, and I am tied there by the affairs of my Order, as the Grand Master has been so kind as to put me in charge of them here, to deal with the Republic.'[11]

At the same time, he was proving that he had retained much of what he had seen and heard during his long European tour. Venice was a listening post and a useful place to be in. Sagramoso managed to uphold the Order's privileges against Austria's encroachments, and he also tried to send out feelers into the Near East. He did not attempt to study Turkey's military preparations: Turkey was no longer a threat. But trade with the east was of increasing importance.

Grand Master Pinto realized that Sagramoso was one of his most gifted Ambassadors at a time when difficult negotiations were in progress. To begin with, Frederick II was pressing for a recognition of the Protestant Grand Priorate of Brandenburg and the confirmation of his brother Ferdinand of Prussia's election as *Herrenmeister*. Sagramoso was quite in favour of this and did much to bring about the important reconciliation, which took place in 1762.

He was next employed on an even more delicate negotiation. The Order owned a priory in Poland with extensive lands bequeathed by Prince Ostrog. After the first partition of the kingdom, Russia had grabbed the estate, stating provisionally, however, that some sort of agreement was possible. It was a difficult and dangerous negotiation, for Russia had been trying for more than a century to get the Order's support in her attempts to secure a footing in the Mediterranean. Peter I had sent an envoy to Malta, Russian volunteers had served on the Order's ships (and they had been perfectly well-behaved, pleasant young men), and now Catherine II was writing charming letters to the Grand Master, sending him her portrait by Levitzky and also dispatching a fleet to Valetta. She had tried several times to drag the Order into an attack on Turkey.

Sending Sagramoso to Russia was a good start. The Bailly de Mirabeau—a nobleman from Provence and a good naval commander—sought the appointment, but Pinto refused, knowing that Sagramoso would do very well; besides, Sagramoso was younger and stronger than Mirabeau and could better withstand the terrible Russian climate. He proceeded to Paris first, where he saw the Bailly de Fleury, the Order's Ambassador and his life-long friend, and he was given a letter of introduction, his credentials, duplicates of many letters which had already passed on the subject, a code, and various historical and financial notes, for the whole of which he signed a receipt on December 1, 1772.[12] Then he proceeded to London, to settle the financial part of the operation with his banker, Hart, in Sackville Street. When he was clear about the background of his mission, he left for Russia, having been notified to act 'before the Polish cake had been sliced and eaten by the three guests'. He went through Strasbourg and Karlsruhe, and reached Warsaw in January 1773; then he went to Vienna in the same month. Maria-Theresa was utterly charming to him; he was invited to the great State ball, but his Vienna colleagues were not at all helpful.

Eventually he reached St Petersburg in April and things at once became extremely difficult. Not that Catherine was unpleasant: she was rather cloyingly sweet, and Sagramoso constantly felt the ominous presence of some dangerous subject. He could never come to grips with the people with whom he sought discussions. When writing to Fleury to ask for a length of black silk ribbon on which to hang his cross, he added, knowing that his letters were read by the Imperial censorship: 'More than on anything else, I rely on the kindness and nobility of soul of that immortal sovereign.'[13] The Chevalier de Corberon, who was in the French Embassy, met him and wrote in his diary: 'He is a worthy, gallant man, very much versed in philosophy, with the most appealing passion for all that is pleasant in life.' Once more, Sagramoso was displaying all his charm. Another diplomat liked him very much; the Duke of Serracapriola, who was the Neapolitan Ambassador.

After some desultory talk, he left for Warsaw, unable to stand the Russian climate any longer; he stayed for about a year in Poland, kicking his heels, negotiating with Poniakowski and wondering how long the solemn joke would continue. He was feeling quite bored and wrote to Fleury after a whole year in Poland: 'My dear friend, I swear to you that I am at my wits' end. More than ever, I long to recover my freedom. Man acts only when induced by ambition or interest. When those two inducements fail, he falls back on sloth and does not exist any longer.' This pessimistic explanation did not prevent him from being very active and in the end he reached an agreement which saved for the Order all that could be saved. He went back to St Petersburg to sign the agreement, kiss Catherine's hand and be presented with a snuff-box with diamonds, and then he drove away like the wind, reaching France by way of Holland. The same year he was raised to the rank of Bailly by Rohan. A few years later he went back to Italy, as the Order's Ambassador in Naples.

He remained the great specialist in all Russian questions and this subject kept him busy until his death, for Russian feelers became increasingly numerous and tenacious each year. Naples was an important place, as the Neapolitan Court was intriguing with Russia. Sagramoso kept the Grand Master informed of what was going on. At one time, in 1784, he had to take a very firm line to prevent Prime Minister Acton from attempting an ominous scheme which would have enabled him to turn the Maltese fleet into an elaborate naval school for

Neapolitan cadets, destroying the Order's independence and sovereignty.

In 1783 Catherine wrote to the Grand Master that she was sending an Envoy to Malta, as her connections with the Order were so numerous and pleasant. Rohan was aghast: this was both distasteful and dangerous, for the man was likely to spy on behalf of Naples. The Grand Master called on Sagramoso for help. There was nothing to be done but wait. Rohan was hoping that the scheme had been dropped, when he suddenly heard that Count Psaro, the Envoy, was in Venice. Rohan still hoped that he would go to Naples on the way, and he wrote an urgent letter to Sagramoso, imploring him to see the Russian and probe him, but Psaro suddenly landed in Malta, having sailed down the Adriatic without calling at Naples. The Grand Master wrote to the French Foreign Secretary that the man had arrived 'in the most revolting *négligé*': obviously, he had called on the Grand Master, draped in his boyar robes, covered with fur and embroidery. Rohan took this costume for a dressing gown and was indignant.

Psaro started spying for Russia and Naples at once, with the devoted help of the Bailly de Loras. This collusion was later discovered by Dolomieu, but Rohan did not like him and failed to realize how dangerous was the plot Dolomieu had exposed. He complained bitterly to Sagramoso of Dolomieu. The Bailly was still very active in Naples, passing on to Rohan the notes he received from William Hamilton, and countering Acton, who was always plotting against the Order. He also went for some time to Rome to discuss various matters with the Holy See. Rohan was delighted with his ambassador, an intelligent, active man, full of charm and tact. He was still very good-looking and had a most sentimental intrigue with Countess Sylvia Cartoni-Verza. His biographer insists that the Bailly was a most religious man. It is quite possible, though some of his remarks to Fleury do not agree with this view.

His greatest preoccupation was Russia, but he had other matters to look after. When Rohan organized the new Anglo-Bavarian Langue, a step which called for much diplomatic discussion, Sagramoso helped him as far as he could. It was endowed with properties confiscated from the Jesuits when their Order had been suppressed and the negotiations were difficult and tricky, as most states wanted to grab the spoils for themselves. When the matter was settled, Rohan warmly thanked Sagramoso for his unwavering help.

Sagramoso worked for the Order till his death. He collapsed suddenly and died on March 9, 1791. His loss was deeply felt by Rohan, who had few good men to help him at a time when the Order's position was becoming very precarious. It was Russia, the enemy whom Sagramoso had always dreaded and fought against, which would bring about the Order's downfall a few years later.

CHAPTER XIV

THE CHEVALIER DE QUINSONNAS

꘎꙰꘎

Few Knights of Malta were interested in literature, though they were put into many eighteenth-century novels, being picturesque and unconventional; in the Abbé Prévost's best-known novel, *Manon Lescaut*, for example, des Grieux is a Knight of Malta. Yet there were a few Knights who took to writing, and although none of them achieved any lasting literary fame some were fairly well known at the time. One of these was the Chevalier de Quinsonnas.

He was born in Dauphiné in 1719. His family, the Pourroy de Quinsonnas de Lauberivière, owned several castles and large estates around Grenoble. They were four brothers, one of whom became the Bishop of Quebec; two others went into the Order of Malta. François-Zacharie was the youngest and was known in his family as 'the little Knight'. The brothers were lively, unconventional young men. The elder Knight, Pierre-Emmanuel, fought a case against the Parliament of Grenoble: he had been censored because he had gone to take the Communion, wearing his sword. He was told that it was disrespectful, but he put forward his point that 'a knight's sword is an essential part of his dress, which cannot be dispensed with, even when going to take the Sacrament or when entering a court of justice'. He won his case.[1]

The two brothers had literary tastes and they were both acquainted with writers of repute. In 1738, one of the leading Lausanne divines, Jean-Pierre de Crousaz, received a letter from a young Knight of Malta: it had taken about six months to reach him. The Knight was François de Quinsonnas and he explained to Crousaz that his translation of Pope's *Essay on Man* had brought him back to intellectual life. When he was a child, his family had taken great pains to estrange him from literature: he was to be a sailor and nothing more. We have seen that that was often the case with children who 'had received the Maltese Cross almost in their cradle', as the Abbé Prévost puts it in one of his novels. Quinsonnas went on to say that, now the spell was broken, he was going to devote more time to study, despite the fact that he had still one or two caravans to go through. He was delighted to have at last 'the opportunity to study and be enlightened by a true, wholesome moral teaching'. De Crousaz answered very kindly, offering advice. Eventually he came to know the whole family and the elder brother sent him news of the 'little Knight' when the latter was too busy or too far away to write.[2] The young man was also an officer in the French Royal Navy and it was in that capacity that he went to Constantinople with Castellane, the French Ambassador, and possibly met Sagramoso.

Back in France after a few years in Malta, François de Quinsonnas continued to write to de Crousaz, but his letters have been lost. He seems to have been a pleasant, witty, affectionate youth. He contributed for some years to a literary magazine, the *Spectateur Littéraire*, and became acquainted with Voltaire. Later on they quarrelled, which was a not unprecedented occurrence. His literary efforts are not outstanding. He wrote very poor verse about the battle of Fontenoy, praising the King and the Dauphin for the very active part they took in the actual fighting. His other poem on the subject has an ingratiating aspect: it is semi-comic and the author candidly confesses that he realizes he is not particularly gifted:

'Grand roi, tu sais bien vaincre, et moi fort mal écrire.
*Le plus cheri des rois est le plus mal chanté.'**

When the battle took place, Quinsonnas was in Versailles and not in Flanders. Later on, he decided to write an epic about a very big subject: *The Universe*. 'His poem could have three hundred thousand cantos. It seems that he wants to be the Knight Errant of Truth,' wrote Voltaire, to whom Quinsonnas had confided his hope of writing the greatest of French

---

* 'Great King, thou knowest well how to vanquish thine enemies, but I do not know how to write about it. The best-beloved of kings is the most badly sung.'

epics, and he had books posted from Geneva to Malta, as he needed a certain amount of literature to describe what the Universe was, or should be. Needless to say, it was never completed.

In 1750 Quinsonnas was in Italy, the hero of a rather confusing story. At that time Lady Mary Wortley Montague was on the northern part of the country with her rather shady *cicisbeo*, Ugolino Paluzzi. He was thirty-four and she was sixty-one. She had just been very ill and was convalescing in her house at Gottolongo, not very far from Brescia. It had already been rumoured that Paluzzi was shutting her in, the better to seize her money and her jewels. It may be that he was not her lover, not because of the great difference in their ages, but because his tastes were different. Early in June 1750 Quinsonnas was given an introduction to her by Mrs Anderson and he went to Gottolongo to see her. The reason why he wanted to meet her is not known. What happened there is very obscure. According to Lady Mary, a strange man she had never seen called on her with a letter of introduction from a lady whose very existence seemed very doubtful. She refused to see him; he made a scene, produced a pistol and had to be ejected. This unsavoury young man had already been locked up in France at his father's request. She expressed the hope that he would soon be expelled.[3]

As for Quinsonnas's account of the same episode, it verges on the detective novel, which does not mean it is not true. When he called on the lady, he was immediately surrounded by eight or ten excited people who compelled him to walk to a nearby house where he was given some dinner. Everybody was clamouring for his letter of introduction. He refused to surrender it, though he was threatened with being hanged if he did not do so. He was then shown a pistol—which is exactly the reverse of Lady Mary's version—and locked up for about two hours. Then Ugolino Paluzzi arrived in person and forcibly seized the letter. Quinsonnas had to surrender it, feeling by that time quite frightened and wanting above all to escape from such a gang of lunatics.

He was then released and ordered to proceed at once to the next village, Caretta. He tried to explain that he was bound for Brescia, but he was ordered to do as he was told, or he would be despatched at once to a much less pleasant place, and Count Ugolino summoned two armed men to accompany him to the outskirts of the village. Night had fallen and he managed to give them the slip and reach Brescia by another road. There he lodged a complaint.[4]

He then heard that Lady Mary had also lodged a complaint and was told of the unpleasant way in which she had described him. She apparently wanted the local authorities to take action against him, and she believed, or pretended to believe, that he had been sent out by her husband and daughter to murder her.

The Chevalier was furious and indignant at these suggestions. It seems that Lady Mary continued for several weeks to accuse and abuse him, and what he most resented was being called an adventurer without birth or breeding.[5] Lady Mary was completely demented or, more likely, completely under the spell of her *cicisbeo*, who got her to do anything he wished. Yet, after the Quinsonnas episode, the Brescia authorities thought that the whole matter sounded very strange and a magistrate came to Gotolengo on June 23rd to interview her and find out whether it was true that Ugolino Paluzzi was keeping her as a semi-prisoner. She repeated the excited denials she had formulated in her letters of complaint against the Chevalier, and, a few days later, she was formally invited by Ugolino's mother to publicize the fact that they were on the best possible terms. It does not prove much, as the old countess was certainly her son's accomplice.

By that time Quinsonnas had left Italy and returned to France. A few years later, in 1751, Voltaire described him in a letter to Frederick II as 'the man who probed Lady Mary Wortley Montagu's nature', a proof that the Italian episode was well known. What happened next to Quinsonnas is not known, but in 1757 Pinto, writing to the Bailly de Froullay in Paris, was bewailing the Chevalier's riotous life, not hoping for a more discreet life later on, 'as one does not change at that age'.[6]

Quinsonnas died in Rome in 1759 when he was just under forty years of age.

Self portrait by de Favray

10. Count Michele Sagramoso (artist unidentified)

Grand Master Emmanuel Pinto de Fonseca, by de Favray

11. Grand Master Antonio Manoel de Vilhena

CHAPTER XV

A SWISS KNIGHT OF MALTA
FRANCIS JOSEPH GRISET DE FOREL

⊰✥❀✥⊱

THE most unlikely members of the Order of Malta were the Swiss Knights. The complicated status of their country made life very difficult for them. In 1626 the Grand Prior of Germany succeeded in making Grand Master Vasconcellos sign a decree, according to which the Swiss Knights were compelled to lodge their proofs of nobility with the Langue of Germany. This was very unpleasant for several reasons. One was the fact that they were required to produce a much greater number of quarters than the French or the Italians. Yet no one protested forcibly enough and the decree became one of the basic regulations of the Langue of Germany. Cottoner, who was a faithful retainer of Austria, confirmed it and made the Swiss very angry, the more so as they were often French-speaking and in the service of the French army. German Knights went out of their way to make themselves thoroughly unpleasant to their colleagues. In Valetta they would refuse access to the Auberge d'Allemagne to Knights who were not vassals of the Holy Roman Empire: the Swiss were not, for the Cantons had forcibly broken with the Empire in 1291. Consequently they had to be housed elsewhere —usually at one of the French Auberges—and there were a few violent episodes.

Things became worse when a Swiss Knight was entitled to one of the high dignities of the Order; then quarrels took place and raged all over Europe, bringing in the Empire, the King of France, the Most Worthy Cantons and a few more exalted beings, among whom of course was the Grand Master. Tempers were frayed in the process. There had been several lively episodes in the seventeenth century and the situation grew even worse in the eighteenth.

In 1722 a young nobleman from Fribourg made applications to join the Order of Malta. His name was Francis Joseph de Griset de Forel, the son of Nicolas de Forel and Marianne de Boccard. His family had acceeded to nobility in 1541, and bought the estate of Forel some fifty years later. Even the most drastic German regulations could find no fault with it. His titles were of sufficiently long standing to be accepted by the Order. The Forels were a pleasant, affectionate family and Francis wrote charming letters to his father and his young brother, though it seems that the oldest was a sour fellow. When he heard of his father's death he was quite heartbroken and wept long; and yet he was thirty-six at that time.

The whole family wished him good luck in his attempt to join the Order, and his father gave him some sound advice. In order to please God—and also the Grand Master—and work his way to salvation and a commandery, he was to be humble, polite and a good musician.[1] A few months later Francis was accepted into the Order and had to proceed to Malta forthwith. The whole family dissolved in tears and entrusted the young man to the care of the Virgin Mary and various saints. A few cryptic sentences in one of his letters hint at the fact that German Knights had done all they could to oppose him. The Comte de Forel was hoping to enlist on his son's side the help of their cousin, Claude de Duding, Bishop of Lausanne: he was bitterly disappointed. The Bishop did nothing to help, and two of his nephews, Claude and Jacques de Duding, who had already joined the Order, proved to be their cousin's bitterest enemies.[2]

Such was the situation when Forel left for Malta in 1722 to make his caravans. He took a long time over the usual process and was not a professing Knight before 1731; afterwards he remained in Malta, waiting for promotion, the command of a galley and then the God-sent Commandery which would give him the means to live in comfort on the Continent. Not in Fribourg, though he was born there, for the place did not appeal to him very much: he had a number of unpleasant relatives who had slandered him in his home town.

Malta was pleasant and life was far from dull. He had a few lively quarrels to keep him busy. He was on very bad terms with most of his countrymen, including his cousins Duding and the two Schönaus, uncle and nephew. The uncle was a bore and the nephew a rake, and a dull one, which was worse. Forel got heavily in debt and, in order to make some money, organized a thriving trade, exporting corn to the Continent and importing Swiss cheese provided by his brother.[3] It was strictly against the vow of poverty, but it was sanctioned, or at least tolerated, by the Grand Master: Knights had to live somehow!

Grand Master Vilhena was old and ill. It was obvious that he would not last much longer, and jealousy was rampant. Many Knights wanted to secure some privilege from him before it was too late. Vilhena passed over Forel, giving to a younger Knight the galley to which he felt entitled. Forel was furious, of course, and tried to forget his frustration by living a very gay life during the long Maltese carnival of 1735. It was a good season, with several Italian operas with an all-star cast; it must be remembered that Forel was a keen musician.[4] Then, in spite of his cousins' intrigues and bribes, in June 1736 Vilhena granted him his long-coveted galley at last. It was a great day for him, yet, owing to the very bad financial management of the Order, he had to assume the burden of paying for the ship's equipment. This very questionable custom led to the fact that galley captains hardly ever cared to retain their command for a second term of office, and that the whole staff changed every other year. The only stable officer was the chief NCO, who was practically in command all the time.

However, Forel was immensely pleased. As his second officer he took a Savoy Knight, the Chevalier François de Blonay from Evian, who was twenty-four;[5] a few years later he got himself excused from his vows to marry Nicole de Virieu. Forel reorganized his crew and staff, stocked his ship, secured a first-rate cook and sallied forth intent on getting money back out of prizes. His first campaign lasted forty days and was very successful. He fought against a Turkish galley, conquered it and had to go into quarantine on his return, as there was always a danger of catching the plague. 'Lice, fleas and various bugs were eating us alive,' he wrote to his brother.[6] To while away the time, he organized a good chamber music trio with a harpsichord, a lute and a bass viol, and each evening, when guests had left and they had said their prayers, there was a concert on deck in the cool, starry Maltese night.[7]

His second cruise took him to Egypt. He was in the squadron of Commander de Wignacourt, General of the Galleys. They were first briefed to Oran to help the Spaniards who had just reoccupied the city (they had lost it in 1707), but their orders were changed at the last minute and they were dispatched to the Nile Delta, as Turkish ships were meeting there. The Malta squadron arrived at flood time, and Forel was much impressed by the sight.[8] There were violent fights all along the coast and several galleys were captured, looted and burnt. Forel behaved extremely well and no doubt collected valuable spoils. He demurely wrote that success had been granted him by Our Lady of the Hermits, to whom he was particularly devoted. Back in Malta, with his sea spoils and the help of a merchant from Marseille who lent him money, he restocked his ship and ordered gorgeous uniforms for the crew. Yet nothing was settled about his future. Vilhena was still very ill, though 'he might be play-acting', according to Forel.[9]

Lively rivalries raged in Valetta while Vilhena was now obviously dying, and Forel's letters provide a good insight into the secret workings of the Order. Two candidates were competing for the Grand Mastership, Grand Prior Despuig of Majorca, a Spaniard, and Bailly Pinto de Fonseca, a Portuguese. Both were rich, elderly and busily collecting votes. Forel was for Despuig, but his well-hated cousins, the Dudings, 'sold themselves to Pinto like pigs for 5,000 scudi', and the equally hated Schönau—the nephew—was trying some clever piece of blackmail, working both ways.[10] Eventually Vilhena died on December 12, 1736, and things grew very lively indeed. The departed Grand Master was driven in state to St John and laid to rest while the harbour was closed and the Knights gathered in a conclave in the tower chambers of the great church. Bargaining then began in earnest and Despuig was elected: Forel was delighted. The new Grand Master sent for him. According to Forel, Despuig was already in odour of sanctity. Patience was apparently one of his main virtues. He told Forel 'he owed him the honour which had been bestowed upon him when he was elected, so that (Forel) knelt and kissed his hand and begged him to confirm the privileges he had been granted by the departed Grand Master, which were publicly granted forthwith'.[11] And that was all. No commandery was mentioned and Forel was warned that his cousins were in league with the German Knights and had sworn that, so long as they were alive, no Fribourg Knight would be promoted.

He plied his way backwards and forwards between Malta and Sicily, spending much time on his ship and more or less recouping himself by the spoils. The commander of the Grand Master's galley, with whom he had close relations, was a Chevalier Ruffo, 'a young nobleman equally lacking in experience and in brains, who had been given his command to please his family'.[12] Forel was obviously getting sour. There were other annoying details: with the Spaniards in Sicily, it was almost impossible any longer to make much profit, which meant that he would have liked to do a little more smuggling. Everything was taxed. He had just managed to buy 800 measures of oil for re-export, and everything was becoming expensive and difficult.

Yet life was not always dull. Forel was now thirty-six; he was tall, good-looking, with a well-deserved reputation for being a 'gallant Knight' and, whether in Palermo or Naples, was far from being despised by the fair sex. Once he gave a party on board for Mme Litieri, wife of the Governor of Syracuse, a beautiful Fleming who had not succumbed in the least to Spanish haughtiness. On another occasion, in Trapani, eight ladies came on board with their retinues. They were young and lovely and they organized a pleasant surprise-party.[13] In April 1736, in Palermo, the Malta Squadron was entertained with the greatest magnificence by the Viceroy; they were given the viceregal coaches to ride in and Forel, who was already well known, became even more popular. A number of ladies of high rank had a party on his ship, among them was a Princess Spada Fora, Duchess della Grotta Campofranco and Marquesa Garatana, who became Forel's favourite guest and probably more than that.[14] The next day he formally entertained them on board again and there was a ball which went on until six in the morning. This time the ladies brought their husbands with them.

This life continued for months. It was pleasant, of course, but it was very expensive too, and no Commandery was forthcoming—'the Commandery of which I am more enamoured than of any Palermo princess or marchioness', he wrote to his brother.[15] His father had died, and on hearing the news he had wept bitterly in the arms of his dear friend de Blonay. His export and import trade was bringing in some money, but it did not amount to much. He had an old uncle in Fribourg who was on the point of death, but had been there for ages already. Forel was trying to get some money from a Swiss cousin, Mlle de Forel, to whom he gallantly sent a ring with a serpent's eye and some earth from St Paul's cave in Medina, to protect her from snake bites. Simultaneously he suggested that she might bequeath him one of her estates. How she reacted to such a tactful suggestion is not known.[16]

The situation was so enervating that Forel thought of leaving Malta and entering the Neapolitan service. The King of Naples was about to raise a Swiss regiment, and Forel called on the Infant Don Carlos, who received him extremely well but remained vague as to military prospects. He told him only that applications should be made through the Swiss Canton of Uri, which was very slow to react to anything. Then, if Forel wanted a commission, he had to apply to Uri again. Forel had the greatest difficulty in keeping his temper.[17]

But luck turned at last: the Grand Master, having kept him dangling for months, granted him the Commandery of Alsace; the everlasting uncle died and so did Mme de Forel. Francis de Forel had achieved his aim in life and could repay some of his debts. To make things even more pleasant, the hated Dudings, who had been the bane of his life, had lost any hope of being promoted for a long time, as there were so few commanderies for Swiss Knights. As soon as possible, Forel relinquished his command, called on everybody to receive their congratulations and to say goodbye and left, first for Fribourg and then for Alsace.

His life was not going to be much easier, but he had left Malta in good time, for shortly afterwards Despuig died and his former rival, Pinto, was elected to Grand Mastership and remained in charge until 1772, when he died at the ripe old age of ninety-two.

Forel's commandery was one of the problems of the Order.
It belonged to the Langue of Germany, though it was on
French territory. Estates were scattered over three or four
towns, one of which, Mulhouse, was a free city, more or less
allied to the Swiss. Of the other places where the Order owned
land, only one, Soultz, was Roman Catholic; Colmar and
Mulhouse were Protestant. There the Order dealt through a
local agent who was Protestant. When the Commander visited
his estates, he stayed in Soultz. So did Forel when he went
there in 1757, and he liked the food very much. At one time
his agent in Colmar supplied him with Munster cheese and
Alsatian wine.[18]

Having left Malta and examined his situation, Forel realized
that he could not live in idleness, either in Fribourg or in
Soultz, small towns both of them, which gave no scope to his
activity. Then in 1743 he was appointed tutor to the Elector
of Saxony's son, Xavier, and went to live in Dresden. He was
adequately paid, 2,400 *écus* a year, and well received at court.
The Elector was very pleasant when Forel was presented and
had given him a gold snuff-box. Forel, on the other hand, had
presented the Elector with cheeses; he must have been a
specialist in the matter. Life in Dresden was pleasant enough,
though his pupil contracted smallpox and was almost despaired
of. But such a gratifying state of things could not last for ever.
Saxony was invaded by Frederick II, the Elector fared very
badly, disasters piled on disasters, and Forel was eventually
pensioned off in 1748.

The Commander had come to a dead end once more. He
made a half-hearted attempt to enter the Church, on condition
that he would be appointed Bishop of Lausanne as soon as he
had been ordained. While violently denying this, he tried and
failed: his Malta enemies banded against him and got someone
else appointed instead. By that time Forel had lost all interest
in the scheme and was turning his interests back towards the
Order of Malta.

He had settled in Soultz and was also Receiver for the
Langue of Germany, and because he wanted to enter the
Council of the Langue the old rivalry between Swiss and
German Knights flared up again. The situation became so in-
volved that the Swiss Cantons tried to avoid committing them-

selves. Consequently, Forel applied to Versailles for help and
the Baron of Zurlauben, Colonel of the Swiss in the French
service, sent him advice and agreed that he was perfectly entitled to the post in the Langue of Germany.[19] Forel eventually
secured entry into the Council of the Langue, but his troubles
were not ended and he tried to come to some clear understanding of the situation.

He was lucky again, for the Elector of Saxony had died by
that time and his former pupil's brother succeeded. He asked
Forel to return at once to Dresden, which he did, fighting a
duel before going. For the next twenty years he lived an
interesting life there as Minister and Court Marshal with
baronial status. Prince Frederick died shortly after his arrival
and was succeeded by Prince Xavier, Forel's former pupil.
Forel proved to be a good and clever administrator with
modern ideas about government, interested in social reform,
and very friendly with liberal-minded writers like von Bork
or Hohenloe, who were disciples of the French philosophers
and economists. So much so that part of his Fribourg family
quarrelled with him, though he had taken one of his nephews
with him. Both men had many friends among the foreign
diplomats and were among the most cultured people at court.

Francis de Forel had lost nothing of his fighting spirit. His
high position at court and his devotion to a young sovereign
gave him an even greater will to make his point. This time the
point was the Grand Priorate of Brandenburg, which fell
vacant in 1774 when the elder Schönau died. It was an exalted
position and a revenge that would be sweet.

So Forel set to work, and for ten years he spent his time and
his energy working out his case. Germany was against him.
The new Grand Master of Malta, Emmanuel de Rohan, was
for him, and the Swiss were more or less neutral. In 1776 he
went to Vienna in great state, met Emperor Joseph II, who
was charming, walked with him before the whole court, entertained him and eventually suggested that he should apply to
the Aulic Council! The Ambassador of Malta, Bailly Col-
loredo, presented him to the Empress. How well Forel knew
those pleasant, useless interviews! He received a soothing,
helpful letter from Rohan, who bitterly criticized the Emperor's dilatory attitude, waited for official documents and

suggested a way out of the worst problems. The Swiss Cantons should apply to have their Knights listed in the Langue d'Auvergne instead of the Langue of Germany: that might have been a good solution.

A year later the Grand Prior of Germany, Baron von Reuchning, died. Forel at once applied to succeed him: though he was now seventy-five years old, nothing could tame him. Again he was notified that he had to wait until the Aulic Council had reached a decision. He answered at once that, whatever the decision might be, he could not and would not accept it, and Rohan made the same answer. Another dead end had been reached.

Life continued in Dresden. Forel's pension had been raised to 36,000 *écus*. The young Elector kept him very busy. One of the Dudings had died in 1766, as Commander of Fribourg, and his brother had been given the Commandery of Worms, but Forel had possibly forgotten, if not forgiven, them. Blonay did not die until 1780, having begotten ten children.

Finally, before anything had been decided about his bailly-ship, or a Grand Priorate, Forel died of a stroke in 1786 and was buried in Freidrichstadt.

CHAPTER XVI

AN EIGHTEENTH-CENTURY VIRTUOSO
COMMANDER DE MONTS DE SAVASSE

⇥⟨⟨⟩⟩⇤

A T A TIME when the Order had lost most of its religious impetus, some of its members developed new and occasionally unexpected tastes. Some of them became virtuosi. Malta is one of those Mediterranean territories over which civilization has moved backwards and forwards from time immemorial. Prehistoric temples, a few remains of Greek art, numerous Roman relics, Arab destruction and Norman architecture give the island the appearance it had when the Order took possession in 1530. Hardly any archeological work was carried out, of course, but a few cultured men were attracted by what could still be seen. Most of the temples were half buried, the underground shrines were unknown, but what was there was strange enough. Moreover, cruises aboard the Order's ships took the Knights to some of the Mediterranean sanctuaries—Syracuse, Segesta, Selinontium, Trapani, Naples, Paestum, the Greek islands. At a time when the worship of Greek and Roman antiquity was supreme, when Pompeii was slowly and badly excavated, when Winckelmann was discovering Herculaneum, Malta was in the very centre of the historic area.

Young men who came there for their caravans and subsequent service had much free time, and the most active and intelligent of them put a finishing touch to their often scanty education. Eighteenth-century travellers had a passion for coins, intaglios and, later, geological specimens. At the end of the century the fashion changed and scientific gadgets of the most primitive kind had to be inspected and described: nothing of the sort was ever to be found in Malta, of course, but there was enough evidence of older civilizations to keep specialists interested. Several members of the Order succeeded

138

in combining a military and a scholarly career.

One of these was Félicien de Monts de Savasse. He was a Knight of Auvergne, the eighth and penultimate child of Scipion de Monts, Lord of Savasse, and his wife, Anne de Blanc de Blanville. He was born in 1700 in the Chateau d'Armanais, near the Côte-St-André in Dauphiné. All his life he was to remain on the best possible terms with his brothers and sister and their numerous children. Scipion and his wife brought their family up well and spared neither trouble nor money to provide them with a scholarly education. Even the prospective Knight of Malta was taught Latin and Greek, which was quite unusual. Félicien studied first at home under a private tutor, a very good one; then he was sent to school at Grenoble. He was a clever boy with an eager, intuitive mind, and he found adequate teachers in his school. He became a good latinist, which was frequent in the eighteenth century, and an equally good hellenist, which was quite unusual, even among scholars. It seems that no branch of science was strange to him, for throughout his long life he displayed a lively interest in history, heraldry, archeology, geology, numismatics and a few other things. He was a voracious reader and displayed a many-sided, active, appealing personality.

His uncle, Jean-Baptiste de Monts, a Commander of Malta, got two of his nephews into the Order as 'members of a family well known to the Order'; Félicien, who joined it when he was nineteen, and Louis-Joseph when he was thirteen. The younger one died in Valetta when he was twenty-six. Félicien made his caravans and was received as a professing Knight in 1723.

For ten years he sailed in the Order's galleys and led a not uneventful life. He was a profuse, colourful letter-writer, and in his correspondence once can find vivid sketches of the life of an eighteenth-century Knight. Savasse apparently liked the sea and did not mind her rougher moods. Naval activities interested him and so did his companions. He fought under the Bailly de Langon and met several interesting colleagues; one of them was a Chevalier de Rochechouart, 'as lean as delightful',[1] Later, he wrote that he had met in Sicily the rather unconventional Comte de Bonneval, 'a colonel in France, then a general under the Emperor, and now in

Turkey, where he has assumed the turban to crown his follies and his lack of religion; he has barely missed losing his head. The Turks blame him for the loss of the last battle, in which he commanded the artillery, so that, to avoid their anger and recover public trust through an obvious display of religious feeling, he has made a vow and implored Mohamed to grant him better luck against the Persians,' Savasse wrote to his mother. 'Would to God that his military failures bring him back to duty, making the Turks the first instruments of His wrath! In Sicily I often lunched with this unlucky fellow on board the Bailly de Langon's galley.'[2] Savasse sailed over the greater part of the Mediterranean, and saw all he could of the remains of former civilizations, and started collecting coins, a hobby in which he was to become a specialist.

This was not only on account of his very genuine passion for Greek and Roman coins: they could be bought by the bucketful, sorted out and resold at a high price to collectors. Throughout his life, Félicien de Monts de Savasse did make and sell selections of coins, and we shall see some surprising results of his useful activities. Like most young Knights of Malta, he had only very scanty financial resources. He had relinquished all his worldly possessions to his widowed mother for a monthly allowance which she hardly ever paid. The Countess de Monts was squandering the family estates on various priests, nuns and monks, to the fury of her children, who could not get a penny out of her and had to borrow money at extortionate rates.

Félicien had enlisted another, and more active help, Mlle de Tambonneau, the sister of a Commander of the Order. She was older than himself, rich, cultured and a blue stocking: 'This young woman preferred to marry books rather than bestow her fortune on some wretched Gascon younger son,' Félicien wrote.[3] Whatever the relations between the elderly Mlle de Tambonneau and the youthful, good-looking, dashing Félicien, she helped him, entertaining him when he was in France, sending him presents, money and jewels when he was in Malta. He used one of her jewels—a topaz set in gold—to bribe the Grand Master.

For Félicien was facing the usual problems of all young, ambitious Knights: trying to get, first the command of a galley, then a Commandery. Just like Griset de Forel, he was trying to extract something from the tight-fisted Vilhena, who had evolved a faultless technique for keeping everyone dangling. He had actually promised a galley to Félicien when the Chevalier de Saint-Simon rushed into Valetta, having attended a conclave in Rome. He threw himself at the Grand Master's feet, wept and stormed, swearing that he was penniless (which was true) and that the command of a galley was for him a matter of life and death. So Vilhena granted him his command and summoned Félicien, to whom he was most charming, laid his hand on his shoulder, said that he loved him as dearly as his own son, and promised him the first free Commandery. Félicien waited for two more years until the word galley 'made him blush to his eyes and become feverish', he confessed to his brother.⁴

He had been given various secondary commands at sea and on the island: he was Major-General in battle, which gave him the commands of two commandos of Knights, organized in case of a Turkish landing. He was also in command of the Fort St Paul.

At last, in 1732, he was placed in charge of the *St Anthony*. He spent all he had in equipping the ship, running heavily into debt, just as Forel had done, merely to realize, just as Forel had done, that he could not recoup himself through smuggling, since the war that raged over Europe made things too difficult.

He tried to bribe the Grand Master in a new way: he ordered a bronze statue of Vilhena, twenty-two feet high, to be cast and erected within the Fort St Paul. He does not say who was the sculptor, and it proved a very costly undertaking. But it was successful and he duly received a Commandery. Félicien was not present when the statue was unveiled; he had already left Malta. He only had to foot the bill, which added terribly to his already heavy debts. What happened to the statue is not known. Vilhena was gracious enough to acknowledge this expensive flattery by several charming letters to the Commander and his mother.

The scene changed as Félicien de Mont de Savasse left Malta for good and hurried to Burgundy to take possession of his Commandery, Laumusse, near Mâcon. It was a beautiful estate which had been sadly neglected by the former Commander, François de Foucauld de St Aulaire, and the new owner realized that it would be both expensive and difficult to restore it to its former prosperity. But Félicien put all his energy into it, running into further debt to repay former ones, and running his estate to make it pay. All his letters to his family—long, amusing, rambling letters—explain what he had to do: repair the house and the grounds, the walls and the roofs, drain the fields, mend the roads, fell dangerous old trees, replace dead cattle, sow and harvest the fields. He had a vivid imagination and tried everything, including silk-worm breeding. Once there was a serious fire at Laumusse, in which several cows died. The Commander bewailed the accident as a major tragedy and succeeded in extracting a large sum of money from the Order to repair the damage. One even feels that he had magnified his losses, possibly becoming a little querulous with old age. In 1764 he was granted a second commandery, Bellecombe in Dauphiné, between Lyons and Bourgoin. The little castle and most of the farms were in a reasonably good state of repair, but the land had been neglected and he had to begin again mending, draining and restoring. Bad years with poor crops, heavy hailstorms, and an outbreak of foot-and-mouth disease worried him very much.

Yet he did not devote all his time and energy to such prosaic work, and till the end of his life he retained a frantic, many-sided activity. His leading passion was numismatics. On his return to France, he went to see President Dugas of the Parliament of Lyons, who described him in the following way: 'He seems a clever man, a virtuoso more than a real scholar and, to be truthful, a man who follows his calling and has spent all his life in voyages and caravans, has no time to go deep into scholarship. He is about forty, as far as I can see. He told me he wanted to sell some of his coins.'[5] Two years later they were bought by the city of Lyons. There were 20 gold coins, 1,672 silver coins, 47 bronze statues, 28 semi-precious engraved intaglios, Egyptian and Roman statues, Greek vases, and Etruscan coins, a really beautiful collection which Félicien had lovingly created during his Mediterranean cruises. Having parted with it, he often bewailed his loss but continued alternately to collect and to sell coins and statuettes.[6]

Then, on March 1, 1764, a hoard of coins and statuettes was discovered in Mâcon by a vintner who was working on the courtyard of the old Hospital. It was 'under a covered path, opposite the middle of the ramparts'. The treasure consisted of silver and bronze statuettes, about 600 coins of the Emperor Gallien's period, a large gold pin, dishes and vases. A lawyer named Aulas grabbed a number of coins, some of them gold, and seven silver statuettes. The vintner had broken a bronze serpent and brought to a local priest a statue of a veiled woman holding a child, which he took for a statue of the Virgin Mary; but the priest told him it was an idol and sold it. Félicien de Savasse heard of the find and hurried to Mâcon: he bought a basketful of coins for three pence. He also acquired from Aulas the statuettes of Mercury, Jupiter, Cybele, Tychee. When, a few years later, the Comte de Caylus compiled his *Recueil d'Antiquités*, he made contact with Félicien, who lent him the statuettes which were engraved and reproduced in his book. Savasse had also a detailed account of the discovery. The statues are now in King Edward VII's Gallery in the British Museum, bequeathed by Richard Payne-Knight, who came by them at the end of the eighteenth century.

Félicien de Savasse did not limit his intellectual activities to archeology. Like most cultured men of his time he dabbled in natural sciences too. He was always interested in 'thunder stones' and had a long and detailed correspondence with various friends about them, begging for chips of a particularly fine one which belonged to a M. de Beost: as its owner regarded this as an uninteresting bit of pyrites, Savasse was quite indignant.

On September 16, 1763, a large stone fell from the sky not far from Mâcon. Savasse heard the noise, and, taking the royal notary with him, he began to investigate the matter thoroughly. They went everywhere, asking questions of people who had heard the sound of the falling stone, and begging them to analyse their impressions. One man was drinking at the local inn, another was fishing, a third was shooting with his bow and arrows. One had fallen down on hearing the noise, which sounded to him like the report of a gun, and an old soldier had said that he took no notice, having been for many years in the army and on battlefields. All had

smelt a nauseating stench of sulphur. All the answers were
recorded most formally. The sound of the fall was described
as 'a fantastic hissing noise, coming after a frightful buzzing
and bellowing, together with sounds like those made by guns,
muskets, drums, timpanies, trumpets, haut-boys, and flutes,
resembling very much those I thought I heard fifteen years
ago, when approaching the Italian volcanoes', wrote Félicien,
summing up the inquiry.[7]

Eighteenth-century scholars were fascinated by volcanoes
and many Knights of Malta had visited Sicily and seen Mount
Etna, or had even ascended it. Anyway, Savasse picked chips
of the splintered stone and started all sorts of chemical experi-
ments on them, grinding them, heating the dust, testing it with
sulphuric acid, hydrochloric acid, vinegar, regal water, or
exposing it to a burning glass which had been lent him by a
friend, the Abbé de la Richardie. Nothing much resulted,
except that he concluded that the stone had first melted and
then solidified again during its fall, passing from an extremely
hot place to an extremely cold one. There is something quite
touching in the slightly clumsy care with which the old
Knight investigated that phenomenon which had taken place
on his doorstep.

Life in Laumusse was not dull, it seems, and Savasse was
never at a loss to enliven it. He had many friends: in his vast
correspondence are mentioned the names of the many people
he visited or received. Among them were various members of
the La Richardie family, including a Knight of Malta, much
younger than himself, who was going through a rather surprising career on the island, Gabriel de Besse de la Richardie.
Another acquaintance was Commander Mathieu Beaulme, an
old man who had been one of the Knights captured at Algiers
in 1707. He had retired to Mâcon after serving as a colonel in
the Emperor's army. He died in 1765 and Félicien could not be
with him at the end, as the weather was very bad and he had
to be careful not to catch cold. Félicien must have been a
pleasant, lively companion, full of humour and able to tell
many stories and tell them well.

He was a charming uncle too. He had two nephews and two
nieces whom he cared for more attentively than did their
parents, who seem to have been lazy and casual. Félicien wrote

12. Grand Master Ximenes de Taxada, by de Favray
Grand Master Emmanuel de Rohan, by de Favray

13. Jean de la Valette and Andrea Doria (by an unknown Italian painter)

Council under Pinto de Fonseca, by Tiepolo

long letters to the children, advising them on many things, from behaviour at meals, to the advisability of studying Latin and mathematics, what to read or how to draw. He told them amusing stories which had a fitting moral. For instance, how a young Knight of Malta, Chevalier Ruffi, arrived in Valetta as one of the Grand Master's pages, speaking no language but a barbarous Sicilian dialect and some bad Latin. As he was an intelligent lad, he realized at once that he had no hope of achieving anything until he rid himself of his unpleasant accent and mastered a few more languages. He worked very hard and in a short time his Italian was faultless and he could also speak good French.[8] Félicien presented the boys with drawing materials and the girls with muffs and ribbons. But his intelligent affection for youngsters went further. His brother did not like to bother about his children and they fared the worse for it. The elder had been sent as a volunteer to the army when he was barely ten: Félicien was indignant and he expostulated with his brother over such barbarous treatment of a child. For his actions the Comte de Monts was also criticized by a much higher authority: the child was already a second lieutenant in his regiment when Louis XV, inspecting the troops, observed the baby-officer and suggested he would be better elsewhere. Accordingly, the child was sent to the Military Academy, where Félicien, who had taken the matter in hand, had got him accepted as a pupil. Yet, a year later, he was again serving in Germany with his regiment.

Félicien knew a great deal about religious orders and did not trust them: he bitterly protested against forced vocations for girls.[9] On one occasion, several nuns had escaped from their convents near Dijon. When he told his brother the story, Félicien made scathing comments about one of them 'who was with child by some despicable third-rate painter', but he was even more indignant at the fate of one nun who had been taken back to her nunnery, where she very soon became mad and died. His nieces had been sent for education to a convent in Grenoble; he observed that 'convents are not a school of life but of death'.[10] He suggested other means of education; he was extremely broadminded and he thought that girls should be taught, not only how to read and write, but to spell correctly (a very unusual idea in France at that time), arithmetic, drawing, music, geography, history, mythology, heraldry and a few other things, to shape ther minds and hearts. He then suggested that the elder sister should be sent to Pantemont, the Paris convent where Mlle d'Orleans was brought up before she married the Prince de Condé.[11] Félicien had connections who could put his niece in touch with the Princess, and he would pay her pension. The parents refused. Félicien then had another scheme ready: he would have the girls with him at Laumusse and teach them himself. He would start with 'coins struck by princes during the last three centuries to commemorate the most important events of their reigns, for their ministers, their generals, scientists, great artists, founders of new religions, and illustrious knaves: the best way to acquire knowledge than by any other means'. The girls would have to know the events that were commemorated, who were the people or families involved, and so on. It would be much better for them than getting bored by playing cards or discussing the latest fashions, and hats with old ladies.

Félicien had also evolved a very clever way of providing his nieces with pocket-money, while interesting them in his beloved coins. In winter, Laumusse could be pretty dreary, especially for young girls, who would be more or less cut off from the world: he then would send them to Lyons to one of his relatives, the Marquise de la Rivière. He had already organized his Commandery to welcome them. Reading between the lines, one detects a passionate craving for the society of young and lively people who would bring some gaiety into the life of an elderly man who was still active and eager for affection. The scheme miscarried because the girls got engaged; then he invited them and their husbands to stay with him. He went on, explaining how much—or how little—he could give the girls, hoping they were marrying nice young men as they[12] were both much too pleasant to waste their lives in dull, paltry chores.

In March 1767, he wrote to his brother, telling him among other things that 'I took down a book full of most interesting and truthful stories, not knowing that a window was open in the next room, and there was a draught through a door left ajar. I caught a cold which first afflicted my throat, then my chest with a horrible cough and fever which turned out to be whooping-cough and I am not yet rid of it, in spite of my having been bled, purged, made to vomit, given herb-tea, clysters, juleps, been wrapped in hot towels and provided with all that doctors can think of under such circumstances, so that I have been for almost three months sitting up in bed, unable to turn right or left, coughing, spitting, sneezing, blowing my nose and always filled with great pains when moved.' Then trouble started with his bowels, as he could not take the amount of exercise he was used to, and he also had trouble with his eyes. It did not prevent him from dictating a forty-page letter to his brother, a sort of apology for his whole life, explaining, among other things, that he was not the spend-thrift he was said to be. It is a charming, witty, lucid letter, and yet one wonders whether he had not realized that the end was near.[13] He more or less recovered for a short time, but he died in April 1768 in Laumusse of a gouty attack (*goutte remontée*) having been unable to carry out most of his histori-cal, scientific and agricultural schemes. He left no will and his financial situation was found to be so involved that both his family and the Order of Malta repudiated his succession. A number of books, Greek and Egyptian coins and books of numismatics and a few glass and earthenware vases were found in Laumusse.[14]

CHAPTER XVII

THE SAD LIFE OF
GABRIEL DE LA RICHARDIE

❦

O F Laumusse, Gabriel de la Richardie was the last
Commander but one. It came to him after Monts de
Savasse's death.

Gabriel's family was very old. They had taken their name
from one of their fiefs as early as 1400. They lived in their
chateau at Aulhat, near Issoire in Auvergne, a harsh and
sombre country where the fortresses and churches are built
with the lava of extinct volcanoes. In 1730 Jean-Eustorge de la
Richardie married Elisabeth de Rouvroy de Saint-Simon: the
bridegroom was thirty and his bride twenty-three. She was
the sister of Claude de Rouvroy de Saint-Simon, who by that
time had been admitted into the Order of Malta after a fairly
riotous youth. Both families were equally noble and equally
impecunious. They had many children, though they did not
live happily ever after, and out of seven sons five were sent
to Malta. Nothing much is known about the Marquess and his
wife but, in the light of what follows, it seems that he was an
unpleasant man.

Their second son was born in 1732 and was christened
François-Gabriel. His life was to reveal his restless, unhappy
and unlucky temper, in harmony with the restless period that
led eventually to sombre romanticism. Not that Gabriel de la
Richardie indulged in any kind of literary composition, but
some of his surviving letters are deeply tragic.

He was received into the Order when he was twenty and
left for Malta. Almost at once he got himself into trouble
of a dangerous and obscure kind. One can only guess the
nature of the outrage he was accused of committing, for
early in 1753 he was in prison in Fort St Elmo and writing to
Pinto:

'My Lord. In God's name, may Your Highness have pity upon me. It is hard to ruin one's health at twenty-two in a prison to which one is so unjustly committed. In my sad plight I cannot refrain from imploring Your Grace, begging you to be kind enough to send to Rome to ask for my pardon.

Le Chevalier de la Richardie.

'I hope Your Grace will be good enough to send a *speronare* to bring it back. Send it at my own expense, if necessary.'[1]

The boy was obviously at his wits' end. Whatever had happened, the tragedy must have been both shattering and sudden. The letter is undated: La Richardie never dated his letters, used no punctuation and scribbled hurriedly, in a forcible and obscure style. By its place in the Grand Master's files, we may reckon that it had been written before the beginning of February 1753. On the 17th his father wrote to Pinto from Aulhat, begging him to safeguard his family honour and 'to have my wretched son, of whose unruly behaviour I have heard, not only under arrest, but confined in the closest possible imprisonment on a bread and water diet; it has driven me mad with rage'. He was sending, almost by the same post, a younger son, a sturdy lad of seventeen, who would 'compensate for the wretch who is in Malta, whom I utterly renounce'. Gabriel must have been guilty, or accused of, some very shocking offence.[2]

Pinto answered neither the father nor the son, and months elapsed. The Marquess wrote again. On September 6, 1753, he told the Grand Master that the King had granted him a *lettre de cachet* to have his son arrested and imprisoned as soon as he landed in France. M. de la Richardie begged the Grand Master to ship the culprit to France, without telling him what was in store for him in Marseille or Toulon. The younger son, Gaspard, had not yet left: he must not run the risk of meeting the black sheep of the family.

M. de la Richardie seems to have been a sly, cruel man. Pinto was not soft either, but he apparently did not like the Marquess's attitude and replied, forbidding him to use his *lettre de cachet*. As for Gabriel, he was still imprisoned in the Fort St Elmo and kept in ignorance of his father's behaviour. The Grand Master did not send him back to France.

At the beginning of 1754, the prisoner wrote to Pinto again: it was an incoherent and despairing letter:

'Your Eminent Highness, you refused to hear me after I had been arrested on your orders, but you must let me tell you how unjust it is to make me suffer, since I am completely innocent. I am told by everybody that Your Highness wanted to send me back to France and that I had begged you to do so. Nothing could be further from the truth, as Your Highness knows well. The main reason why I had to stay here was that I was waiting for my brother, who is coming on the *St Anne*, as I had the honour to tell you. It is a false rumour which is spread by my adversary and it is very hard on me.

'I have always known how just you are, too well to fear that you could inflict such treatment on me; the more so because, were Your Highness to send me away, I would not know what to do or where to go, not daring to face my family with that business on my hands, of course! My father would blow out my brains, and he would be right to have me rather dead than alive and dishonoured. Such is the extremity to which I would be reduced if Your Highness did not do me justice. There would be nothing left for me but to kill myself, or to beg my way from harbour to harbour, seeking the wretch who has brought me here, and to revenge myself. Besides, My Lord, it seems that, making a scapegoat of me is encouraging calumny: were you to send away all those who are accused of theft, everybody would be dismissed and they would then be free to rule Malta. He [Gabriel's enemy] knows very well that, had I sued him in court, he would have been dishonoured long ago. Finally, My Lord, I throw myself at your feet and put my trust in your justice. I am sure you will recognize my good faith and deal with my adversary, who is the culprit, as he deserves. It is very hard that this man pounced upon me at a time when I thought the least of him, and then made my life a nightmare. I trust that the local rumours are idle. I rely on your usual kindness and I have the honour to be...'[3]

This rambling letter must have been penned at one stretch by a man in great terror and completely exhausted. In France his father had not relented. On September 10, 1755, he was writing again to Pinto, complaining that the Grand Master had forbidden him to have his son imprisoned in France and begging him to have Gabriel committed to solitary confinement.

Yet by that time Gabriel had been set free and, despite the father's anger, the whole matter was calming down. One of the strangest aspects of the Order of Malta is the utter indifference with which a spell in prison was regarded by the Knights. La Richardie spoke about 'dishonour': it was not so. He was very young and very lonely and upset: otherwise he would not have taken the matter so much to heart as, in fact, no one did after a while. The years that followed proved perfectly normal and even promising. Innocent or not, he was released, and he took his vows. His brother Gaspard had arrived in Malta, where he made a very fine career. So did Gabriel, who remained on the island and became a good sailor, commanding his own ship.

In May 1769 he brought back a choice prize, laden with coffee and cotton.[4] Overjoyed at this achievement, Pinto appointed him Captain of the Grand Master's own galley, built at his own expense.[5] Quite possibly it was La Richardie who took William Hamilton and Lord Fortrose round the ship when they visited Malta on that same year.[6]

Gabriel went back to sea in September, and at the end of the year he was given the Commandery of Laumusse, where his friend Félicien de Savasse had died the year before. He was thirty-eight.

Shortly afterwards he left Malta and went back to France to take possession of his estate. He probably found it in a very ruinous state: Félicien de Savasse was heavily in debt when he died, and in the interval there had been no money to maintain the property. The woods and the house must have suffered. The estate is a fine one, but with the woods neglected and the little pond green with weeds, a dilapidated house and the ghost of a Knight Templar tapping in the cellar (according to a local legend), it must have appeared rather dreary. The climate was chilly and damp for a man used to the sun and heat of Malta. It seems that La Richardie did not stay long at Laumusse after collecting the rents. In 1772 he wrote to

Pinto, asking permission to join Bailly Gambarena, who was going on an embassy: as usual, the letter is undated, without an address. As he asked the Grand Master at the same time to admit into the Order the son of Count Kesnileff, master of the household of some Royal Highness whose name he does not give, La Richardie was possibly writing from Poland, Denmark or Sweden. One thing is certain: his letter, perfectly calm and friendly, comes from a man who was now on good terms with the Grand Master. He had sown his wild oats and the dark days were over.[7]

Pinto died the same year and La Richardie apparently travelled north. Things went smoothly for a while and then a new crisis developed. On April 2, 1774, the Commander de Laubespin, one of the administrators of the Langue d'Auvergne at its headquarters in Lyons, wrote to the new Grand Master, Ximenes, to let him know that, after numerous complaints from angry auditors, he had been compelled to confiscate Laumusse. No one knew where the Commander was: letters remained unanswered. He may have been in his northern embassy still. The Sacred Council of the Order in Valetta took the matter up. This was a serious offence and they summoned La Richardie to Malta to answer the charges against him within six months. But the summons could not be delivered because he had disappeared, so it was served at Laumusse. The farmer there had no idea where the Commander was.[8]

Somehow, the latter heard of what was afoot: members of the Order saw him later in Metz, obviously returning from Central or Northern Europe. He was travelling hurriedly; he crossed Plombières, in the Vosges, reached Lyons by night, stopped for only a few moments to change horses and then, increasing the pace, raced down the road to Provence, making for Montpellier or Marseille. Then all trace of him was lost. He could not have been arrested in France, for the Order was powerless, except when a complaint, duly lodged with the King of France's parliaments, had been accepted, and that would have taken a very long time. They could only collect evidence against the absconding Commander. One of the chief creditors was a Mlle Ricard, whoever she was.[9]

It is easy to realize what had happened. La Richardie was short of money to maintain himself in his northern embassy; he had borrowed money which he could not repay and he may have mortgaged part of the Commandery, and that was a crime. Why had he returned to France, since he was safer abroad? Here we can only guess. He may have raced back to Laumusse to collect a legacy from Monts de Savasse, which could provide him with some means to live abroad: the seven silver statuettes found by the former Commander in Mâcon. They were famous, having been reproduced in the Comte de Caylus's book, which added to their value, while not making them impossible to sell.

The unlucky man was obviously at his wits' end. He knew he was summoned to appear in Malta and what this would mean. He could not face a second term in prison in Fort St Elmo or Fort Manoel. He was now forty-three and a further and perhaps longer spell in prison would certainly kill him. Ximenes, an elderly Spaniard, was a crueller man than Pinto. He would have no compassion for a man who had embezzled the Order's funds. La Richardie lost his grip and abandoned his past, his traditions, his career. He probably made for Marseille and took ship for England.

He was right not to hope for mercy from Ximenes. In April 1774 the latter wrote to his Ambassador in Paris, the Bailly de Saint-Simon: 'The behaviour of the Chevalier de la Richardie troubles us very much and deserves all our attention. You know that he has thrown himself into the pit.' He had not obeyed the summons to Malta and was leading a wayward life. The Grand Master was contemplating the most stringent measures against him. Ximenes continued: 'Are we going to be compelled to deprive our Ambassador's nephew and Great Equerry's brother of the habit?' He was referring to Saint-Simon himself and to Gaspard de la Richardie respectively. So the Grand Master suggested to Saint-Simon that he should apply for a *lettre de cachet*—again!—and secure La Richardie's arrest in France: the scandal would be less grievous than in Malta.[10]

I have been unable to trace Gabriel de la Richardie in England: he may have gone anywhere and assumed any name. Did he meet Richard Payne-Knight, who was just back from his first trip to Italy, and did he sell him the seven silver statuettes? In Payne-Knight's manuscript catalogue in the British Museum there is no explanation of how he acquired them. Usually he gives ample information about the origin of the coins or statues he bought, and from whom he bought them. Is there a secret here? It is tempting to assume that it was La Richardie who brought them to England.

The price of seven small silver statues would not maintain a man for very long. By September 1775 Gabriel was at the end of his tether once more. Life in exile is hard and he was probably feeling very lonely. In September 1775 his uncle, Saint-Simon, wrote to Malta that La Richardie was in Bordeaux, where he had probably shipped straight from England, waiting for the Order's squadron to take him back to Malta, 'trusting in the Grand Master's mercy'.[11] He actually joined the ships in Spain, where measures had been taken to compel him to board: it seems that he went freely, accepting now a fate from which he had attempted escape a few months earlier. Physically and morally he was broken and could resist no longer.

Yet this time he was lucky. As he was still in Western Spain on October 16, 1775, he probably did not arrive in Valetta before Ximenes' death, which took place on November 9th. Anyhow, on the occasion of a Grand Master's elections pardons were granted, and the new Grand Master, Emmanuel de Rohan, was a generous, compassionate, broad-minded man who certainly saw no reason why he should ruin La Richardie's life. Two things are certain: in 1778, the latter still ranked as Commander of Laumusse on the list of French Knights, and he died in France in 1783 with the same rank. He had been unable to repay his debts and his creditors continued to clamour for payment after his death. His estates had been very badly maintained (he did not die there) and the last Commander of Laumusse, Louis-Antoine de Garrel d'Uzech, hurried there to reorganize the place and find new tenants, then left, as there was no question of living there.

CHAPTER XVIII

WHAT A PUNCH AND JUDY SHOW
CAN LEAD TO
THE CHEVALIER DES ADRETS

❧❀❀☙

OF the terrible personalities who displayed themselves during the religious wars of the sixteenth century in France, one of the most repulsive was the Baron des Adrets, a nobleman from Dauphiné, who was dreaded and execrated both by his enemies and his own party. He was a Protestant but was denounced by both Calvin and Coligny. His three sons, who were as repulsive as their father, died young, unmourned and without issue. One, who had become a Catholic, was one of the murderers of St Bartholomew's eve.

Besides those ungracious sons, the Baron had two daughters. The elder married a Marquis de Vaulserre, who assumed his father-in-law's title after the death of the sons. The Vaulserres des Adrets were Protestants, but they changed their religion during the seventeenth century. At that time they were leading a rather drab and secluded life in their chateau near Grenoble: they were not rich and the Baron's spoils had evaporated long ago. By 1760 his descendant was Apolinaire-Etienne, who had married Marie-Josèphe de Bailly. They had three sons and at least one daughter, who was a canoness of St John. On May 18, 1769, their youngest son was baptized in the Church of St Louis in Grenoble, Pierre-Alphonse, born the day before. Like one of the Abbé Prévost's heroes, he had 'received the Cross of Malta almost in his cradle': he was just under one year old when he was accepted into the Order as a Knight of Minority, thanks to a special Papal dispensation. For some unknown reason, he was admitted into the Langue de Provence while Dauphiné Knights were usually admitted into the Langue d'Auvergne.

Nothing is known about his childhood. Subsequent episodes

allow one to realize that life was far from delightful in the
dilapidated chateau overlooking the valley of the Isère. The
eldest brother was a councillor of the Grenoble Parliament and
the second a page at Versailles. When Alphonse was seventeen
he took ship for Malta for his caravans.

The Grand Master at that time was Emanuel de Rohan,
a pleasant and cultured but rather weak man who was
generous and compassionate, and usually kind to young
Knights whom he often helped out of impossible situations in
which they had got involved. He had been enthusiastically
acclaimed at his election in 1775, but his initial popularity was
dwindling because he was trying to rule the Order, a difficult
undertaking when there were so many impassioned personalities opposing his rule more or less openly.

This was the man whom Alphonse des Adrets was to serve.
He arrived in Valetta at a moment when things were becoming
very complicated and tempers frayed, and when the treasury
was rather depleted. He himself did not prove to be a blessing
or a peace-making factor among his colleagues. The great
dignitaries of the Order were well used to any kind of temper
among young Knights, including the most disconcerting. All
those younger sons, cut off from their families, familiar surroundings and traditions, cooped up in a small, overpopulated
island, where discipline was both strict and vague, were
certainly not in ideal circumstances for leading a quiet and
reasonable life. When they were at sea the rigid naval discipline
kept them from mischief. They amused themselves in the
various ports of call—Palermo, Naples, Lisbon, Toulon,
Barcelona—where their caravans took them. They went from
balls to feasts and to Court receptions. The time of glorious
sea fights was past. In Malta they had any amount of time to
waste; they dragged themselves from one coffee-house to
another, playing billiards or cards, gambling and getting bored.
Besides, Maltese ladies were not straitlaced and temptations
were numerous.

The Grand Masters had realized how unpleasant and even
how dangerous the situation was, and they had provided the
Knights with some healthy pastimes. Large grounds had been
organized in Floriana, just outside the ramparts, where they
could play games and train in the open. In 1731, Manoel de

Vilhena had built a theatre in Valetta, next door to a Carmelite convent. Companies of Knights performed both plays and operas,[1] and the younger men—some of them not above seventeen—took the women's parts. The theatre had a small auditorium painted white and gold, five rows of boxes, stalls and a small, shallow stage. The plays were always a great success and the Knights acted three times a week, sometimes with very few rehearsals, so that the prompter had a very heavy task. Invitations were highly appreciated: Maltese ladies used these occasions as opportunities to display new dresses, for they usually led a semi-oriental life, never venturing out except in their coaches or veiled in black silk *faldetta*. When Roland de la Platière visited Malta in 1778, he admired the dead silence in which the audience listened, so different from the unceasing chatter which went on during the performance of an opera at the San Carlo in Naples! Sometimes there were concerts or puppet-shows.

Young Vaulserre des Adrets arrived Malta, went through his caravans with disgust, and evinced at once a most unpleasant temper in spite of his great youth: his notorious sixteenth-century ancestor had probably left his mark upon his descendant. 'This baby caravanist has constantly behaved very ill since he arrived Malta. He is shockingly noisy and riotous,' wrote the Bailly de Loras to the Bailly de Suffren in 1788.[2] Following upon his victories in India, Suffren had been sent to Versailles as the Order's Ambassador. Charles-Abel de Loras, at fifty-two, was moving heaven and earth to get himself appointed as the Order's Ambassador in Rome. His hard, sly temper had made him many enemies, who in addition were jealous of him because ladies looked on him very sweetly, though he was a hunchback. He behaved with the utmost brutality towards those who were weaker than himself, yet he may not have been unduly hard upon des Adrets, who was certainly not easy to deal with. Rohan was to say that he was restless, undisciplined and noisy. It is obvious that most of his superiors did not like him, but it seems that there was more in him than the bad manners of an ill-behaved boy. His contemporaries accepted him as a leader, and a young Chevalier de Montferré was quite devoted to him.

Trouble broke out suddenly: it began as scarcely more

than a rag by boys who had possibly drunk a little too much. In June 1788, during a Punch and Judy show at the theatre, des Adrets and twenty-six other very young Knights started a row and 'uttered yells which were as violent as they were scandalous', wrote Loras.[3] They objected, they said, to the presence in the stalls of servants-at-arms (low-rank Knights), and they proceeded to kick them out. The servants reacted violently and the whole place became a madhouse in which people fought with their fists and feet, though no one mentions that swords were drawn. To make things worse, this took place before the ladies, who were both shocked and terrified and screamed with excitement. Des Adrets started yelling abuse at one of his colleagues, Le Bon, 'a young, well-behaved youth'. It seems that everybody concerned was less than twenty years of age.[4]

As a matter of course, the youthful gang was arrested and sent to Fort St Elmo to cool down. That was not easy: there was a strong public opinion in Malta and an active brotherhood between Knights of each Langue. No one knew this better than Rohan himself, who, when a Bailly, had taken the lead during similar rows, upholding French Knights against the Grand Master and hurling stones into his windows. He was therefore not unduly surprised when the French Knights demanded the instant release of the young offenders. Des Adrets was set free, to the disgust of Loras, who was for a violent solution, wanting to have him and Montferré struck off. Rohan summoned des Adrets to his palace and berated him thoroughly, advising him to behave better henceforth, look after his manners and spare him [Rohan] the trouble of having to enforce punishment, as it would be worse after a second offence.[5]

Actually Rohan was really imploring des Adrets, for the poor man was a prey to endless difficulties; the situation was darkening in Europe, the Order's treasury was emptying quickly, various Knights were making life a burden for him and he was also going through a sentimental crisis. He was the lover of his own young cousin, Marie de Rohan, who lived in Valetta, and though they both behaved with dignity and discretion, the affair was well known.[6]

Des Adrets apparently understood the situation very well

and saw in it a good opportunity of revenging himself upon the Grand Master. In all the Valetta coffee-houses he made continuous and unpleasant remarks about Rohan, abusing him and organizing a widespread resistance to his orders. Rohan had an adequate secret police and was informed of the young man's pranks. A few days later he had him summoned again to the palace and issued an ultimatum: either des Adrets would take the next boat to France, go back to his father and learn better manners (implying that he might come back later), or be arrested and taken to Fort St Elmo. The boy refused to leave and unflinchingly agreed to go to prison! A few days later, Rohan heard with horror that he had lodged a complaint against him with the Grand Inquisitor on the ground of 'denial of justice',[7] and also because he dreaded to be put on ship against his will.[8] What was worse, the Inquisitor had accepted the complaint.

Inquisitor Manciforte was the representative in Malta of the Holy See and from time immemorial such Ambassadors had been on the worst possible terms with the Grand Masters. The Holy See disliked the great independence of the Order and always tried to interfere with it. Here, therefore, was a fine opportunity to plague Rohan, even if the victim, who would be crushed anyway, was only a child. Manciforte wrote to the Roman Secretary of State, explaining that des Adrets had got himself into a very tight corner, setting great powers in movement on a most trivial pretext.

Rohan was feeling very sorry both for himself and for des Adrets. He explained the matter in great detail to the Bailly de la Brillanne, his Ambassador in Rome. The fact that the Inquisitor had accepted the complaint was unprecedented and insulting: of course, he was trying to undermine the Grand Master's authority. Now Rohan was sure he was right. He had acted on the strength of a decree given in 1644 by Lascaris, and it fitted the case very well.[9] And yet, on reading his letters carefully, one feels that Rohan was restless, infuriated against himself and the rest, too. He implored La Brillanne to let him know what he thought of the whole matter. To make things worse, he did not trust La Brillanne! In Valetta, the Langue d'Auvergne was siding with the young man and Rohan had to keep him in prison. He had sent him to Fort Manoel, on an island in Marsamxett Harbour. He did not dare to have him manacled and carried on board: the scandal would have been too great. Montferré had sided with his friend; he was also in prison and had been unable to make his last caravan. The two boys protested against such measures and lodged appeals everywhere, while Rohan grew obstinate. In October 1788 he wrote a sad letter to his old friend Suffren: 'The little plot set up by the Inquisitor makes me look like a despot, and yet there is nothing so contrary to my temper! But this is just inflicted on me to justify the arbitration of the Roman court.'[10] Suffren died shortly afterwards and Rohan had no one left to confide in.

Rohan would have preferred to pardon the two boys. He did pardon Montferré, who was set free in January 1789, but des Adrets did not relent and Rohan secretly pitied the restless, ardent youth; he was almost terrified by his obstinacy. In his prison, des Adrets was visited by all his young friends and he still poured abuse on Rohan and held forth in a most blasphemous way.

In Rome the lawyer of the Order, a Signor Gamundi, was preparing the case, and by January 1789 he had all his documents ready. Loras was then in Rome on private business, and he managed to go through Gamundi's papers: this was illegal and Rohan, who did not like him, was indignant.[11] All he now wanted was a quick end to a worrying story. There was a decision in March, according to which des Adrets was to leave on the first boat for France. The young man refused to accept and lodged an appeal. Rohan was more worried than ever. The boy was unretrievable: rules and orders meant nothing to him. He had now been in prison for over nine months, simply because he had exchanged a few kicks with various people. Now everything had to begin again.

Finally, on July 18, 1789, Rohan, in a triumphant mood, wrote to La Brillanne:[12] on the 12th the young man had been put on board a ship with strict orders to report to Versailles and tell the whole story to the King, delivering at the same time a copy of the Council's decision and the sentence passed.

As the Bastille had been stormed by the mob on July 14th, and as des Adrets did not arrive in Paris (if he ever went there) before the beginning of August, it is quite likely that Louis

XVI could not care less for an obscure affairs between a Grand Master of Malta and a boy of twenty.

What des Adrets did during the Revolution is not known. In 1789 his father was already dead; his mother and elder brother left France. The boy himself disappeared.

CHAPTER XIX

A PAINTER IN MALTA
COMMANDER ANTOINE DE FAVRAY

~❧❀❧~

THE Order of Malta even had painters among its members. On the whole they are not very well known, apart from Caravaggio, who belonged to it for about a year and left it under a very dark cloud, though he painted several masterpieces while in Valetta, two of which are still there. Another painter-Knight has been unjustly forgotten: Antoine de Favray.

He was born at Bagnolet, near Paris, in 1706 or 1710. He studied under de Troy, and when the latter was sent to Rome in 1735, to assume the direction of the French Academy of Painting, Favray went with him. He painted a number of Italian landscapes and eventually aimed higher. He made an ambitious copy of one of the big paintings of Raphael in the Vatican, the 'Fire in the Borgo'. His copy brought warm congratulations from the Paris members of the Academy of Painting in May 1739, and President de Brosses admired it very much.

Little is known of Favray's life in Rome. However, one may assume that it was carefree and lively, like that of most young artists in Italy in the eighteenth century. Favray was witty and gay, and had many friends. At that time the French Academy of Painting was in one of the old palaces in the Via del Corso. Favray made the acquaintance of several Knights of Malta; there was always a fair number in Rome, and in 1744 his friends suggested that he should go with them to Valetta, for in the island he would find new landscapes, new models and a pleasant life. Since the few lively months Caravaggio had spent there in 1607, and after Mattia Preti's death in 1699, no good artist had set foot in Malta, which accounted for the very bad seventeenth-century portraits of the Grand Masters.

Favray accepted and he found all he had been promised. Grand Master Pinto de Fonseca loved pomp and magnificence, and his taste was good. He received Favray extremely well and orders came to him by the dozen. Favray was made a servant-at-arms, a low-rank Knight which granted him several privileges and saved him the trouble of having to make his proofs of nobility. For one thing, he was entitled to wear the eight-pointed cross. Rohan later requested him to become a professing Knight, and in 1785 he granted him the Commandery of Valcanville, which was one normally given to servants-at-arms.

Soon after his arrival, Favray was commissioned to paint Pinto's portrait, which he did very well. He painted several, in fact, either head and shoulders[1] or full-length.[2] He seems to have been fascinated by the haughty, cold, ironic face and the beautiful hands of the old man. He also painted the two other Grand Masters he knew, Ximenes,[3] with his strange squinting eyes and sly face, and Rohan,[4] with his refined, shy deportment. Knights came to him, and Maltese noblemen too.

His paintings conjure up a strange, cosmopolitan society. Among the several paintings by Favray in the National Museum of Valetta is one of the Bailly de Chambray, a leading naval commander of the Order, who died in 1776 while he was Governor of Gozo: he is shown as large and red-faced, with the iron will of the man who had begun fighting when only thirteen and still one of the Grand Master's pages. He is clothed in black, with the large white linen cross of the Baillys. Another painting by Favray, in the same museum, displays the other aspect of the Order: a young Knight with a long, thin, refined face and sad eyes, absentmindedly playing a spinet: he wears the red coat of the galley officers, and the enamel cross on a black ribbon hangs from his lapel. But one of Favray's masterpieces is his portrait of the Bailly von Schauenbourg,[5] Grand Prior of Germany, who died in Malta and was buried in St John: a massive man in red and gold, leaning on a halberd, a sort of good-natured giant. Another fine achievement is the portrait of Baron Inguanez, a member of one of the oldest Maltese families:[6] dignified, in blue velvet coat over a steel breastplate. Favray was also requested to decorate many churches and some of the chapels of St John and the Archbishop's seminary in Floriana.

He asked to be admitted into the French Royal Academy of Painting in Paris, and in 1763 he sent several paintings to the Paris Salon: 'Inside St John', 'A Maltese Family' and 'Maltese Ladies Paying a Call'.[7] The Bailly de Fleury saw them and wrote to a friend, the Chevalier de Rességuier: 'Among other things at the Salon you can see views of the famous Church of St John and a few Maltese ladies by Favray: they are not too dwarfed by the other paintings. Their veracity has been much admired.'[8] On the other hand, Diderot saw them too and referred to them in a most scathing way in his review of the Salon: Favray, in his view, 'has not the slightest spark of genius; his Maltese ladies are miserable', and his conclusion is: 'I do not know if it was advisable to receive M. de Favray into the Academy for his flat copy [of Raphael's fresco], but once he is received he should be struck off on account of his original works.'

By that time Favray had left Valetta. His roaming tendencies had taken him farther east. In 1761 a Turkish galley, the *Ottoman Crown*, had arrived at Malta, rowing all out. The harbour authorities were staggered at the crew's tale. They had come from Smyrna. The Christian galley slaves had revolted on a Friday, when most of the officers were attending weekly prayers at the mosque. They had thrown overboard the few who remained and made for Malta at top speed. When he heard of the incident, the Sultan was enraged, for similar incidents had taken place a few years earlier. His threats were so violent that France, to prevent serious developments, started negotiation, and bought the ship from the Order in order to restore it to the Sultan. Early in 1762, Count de Moriès arrived in Malta on *l'Oiseau* to collect the galley. In order to soothe Turkish feelings, he was supposed not to take any of the Knights on board, but he made one exception, accepting Favray, who seized the opportunity to travel to Constantinople. He arrived by the end of January and painted the *Oiseau* sailing up the Golden Horn.[9]

For several years he lived at the French Embassy, the most welcome guest of two successive Ambassadors, Vergennes and Saint-Priest. He delighted everybody with his wit, humour and talent. He met the beautiful Greek, Santi Lomaka, who had married Louis de Chénier, the French Consul, and became André Chénier's mother. He painted a number of landscapes and episodes in his own life: 'The Reception of the French Ambassador by the Grand Signior',[10] 'The Tower of the Sweet Waters of Asia', 'The Castles of Europe' and 'of Asia', and two sets of 'Greek Ladies',[11] one of them certainly representing Jewish women. He also painted portraits and two of them are masterpieces: they represent the Count and Countess de Vergennes in Turkish dress.[12] The costumes are gorgeous, ablaze with silk and gold, and the sitters know how well the costumes suit them. He sent some of his paintings to the Paris salons: Diderot saw the 'Audience of the Ambassador' in 1771 and was less peevish than on the earlier occasion: 'There is some effect in this little painting,' he wrote: 'its chief merit is its truthfulness, and there were difficulties to overcome. Also the colour is good, though the composition is bad.'

That very year war broke out in Turkey and Favray left. He took ship to Marseilles, where he made a short stay, then returned to Malta, never to leave it again. Pinto died the following year; Ximenes was elected and was painted by Favray, who also painted the next Grand Master, Emmanuel de Rohan. As the latter was overwhelmed with work, he could only sit during mealtimes, on Thursdays and Fridays, when he had no guest to lunch, and could chat with his painter at leisure.[13] Favray was a pleasant, witty man; some of his letters to a great friend, the Chevalier de Turgot, have been preserved and they are most amusing. He once mentioned the Bailly de Suffren, 'who makes a pretty sight, with the Blue Ribbon on his large belly'. He reminded Turgot of his former love, the Signora Giovanna, who had married and become Marchesa Cedronio: 'She always dissolved into tears when your name was merely mentioned, after you had left Malta.'[14]

Suddenly, the Grand Duke of Tuscany heard of Favray and asked for a self-portrait for one of his galleries. 'I cannot see how they came to unearth me from Malta,' he wrote, and he complied with the Duke's wish, painting himself as an 'Asiatic Philosopher' in 1779. At one time it was suggested that the portrait now at the Uffizi was by Liotard, but the letter to Turgot settles the matter.

There is a strange likeness between the composition of that portrait and Alan Ramsay's 'Jean-Jacques Rousseau', made in 1766 while Rousseau was staying with Hume.[15] Though Rousseau referred to it as the 'frightful portrait', it is one of the best and most attractive likenesses. In both paintings the sitter wears a fur cap and a fur-lined coat; but this is no mere coincidence, since it is probable that Favray's 'Asiatic Philosopher' is a poke on the Rousseau title 'Genevese Philosopher', and his garb must have been copied from Rousseau's celebrated Armenian dress. Favray had certainly not seen the original but it had been engraved in 1769.

In 1777 Favray took a French painter, Jean Houël, round Malta and Gozo; Houël was delighted with this witty and colourful guide.

He was now growing old, yet was not losing his grip of his artistic skill. In 1787 he wrote to Turgot: 'In spite of my weak sight, heavy hand, and tired imagination, I still spend my time doing a few things.' He was at least seventy-seven and the world outlook was rapidly darkening. Shortly before the outbreak of the French Revolution he wrote again: 'This is the century of events. It is coming to its end and so am I, happily. I have a very sensitive nature, and if something happens which can hurt me because it hurts my much younger friends (as, at my age, one must not dread things for oneself), at least I shall not see it.' Turgot died shortly afterwards, but Favray survived him and was still alive when the first tragedies of the Revolution took place in France. He died after 1792: it is not known exactly when, nor where he was buried, as his grave in St John has been lost. In France he was completely forgotten.

Though he was not an artist of first magnitude, he had a great deal of talent. His little scenes, full of close observation minutely rendered, may not have the lightness of touch of the contemporary little masters, French or Italian; painting for members of the Order, he had to select his scenes carefully. As a Knight of St John painting for other Knights, he could scarcely be very daring. His Maltese and Greek ladies are very much dressed and almost veiled, but the paintings are always full of humour and the sitters never look as if they were attending a fancy-dress ball.

Favray painted many religious subjects and could not always

avoid their cold pomposity. 'The Discovery of St Paul's Body' and 'The Burning of the Saint's Body by Julian the Apostat', both in St John, are very dull, in spite of a fine white horse in the latter. In the Floriana seminary a set of frescos escape that cold formality, the best being 'St John and St Paul', 'The Death of St Joseph' and 'The Death of St Francis Xavier'. The saints have virile, tragic faces and in the second painting Jesus grieves over Joseph with a moving and dignified tenderness. In the third, a man in a fantastic red costume, supposed to be Indian, throws a touch of fire into the canvas.

Favray's best achievements are his portraits. I have already mentioned several of his sitters. The 'Pinto' in St John is probably his masterpiece. The old Portuguese, with the large white cross and the ermine lining to his black costume, stands against a dull red and gold background of statues and draperies. The proud gesture of the Grand Master, showing the closed crown which he was the first to wear, is very impressive. So is a smaller painting, in which he is shown half-length, holding the crown as if to protect it. A small unfinished 'Rohan' in a similar costume, displays the model's pleasant and irresolute nature. In his female portraits, Favray knows how to make silk shine, or how to throw a transparent veil over jewels. One of his best achievements is the 'Young Maltese Lady' in the Louvre. He also makes much out of the glossy black silk *faldettas*. Some of his self-portraits reveal his humour at its best. Most of them are not very far from caricature, either the portrait in the Uffizi, or the one in which he is pointing at something with an extended forefinger; both display his long, horse-like face in a most comical way. In his distant island Favray's paintings keep alive the image of a strange world which he painted when it was at the point of death. If only for that reason, the painter's name and work should be remembered.

CHAPTER XX

A GREAT SCIENTIST
THE COMMANDER DEODAT DE DOLOMIEU

≈⊰⊰⊱⊱≈

EVERY year the Dolomites, one of the most fascinating of playgrounds for climbers and skiers, attract thousands of visitors: yet how many of them know the origin of the name for the mountains which have the strange shapes of forti-fied Romanesque cathedrals? Peaks, or even whole ranges of mountains, have often been named after the man who climbed them first, or who discovered them, but that is not the case here. The man after whom the Dolomites were named never set foot in the district, though he knew many other Alpine ranges. What he did was to analyse the limestone they are made of. Thus the rock was named after him by devoted friends and disciples, and the name was then extended to the whole system of mountains in northern Italy where that kind of limestone is found. Unusual as this may seem, the life of Déodat Tancrède de Gratet de Dolomieu himself was far from ordinary.

The eighteenth century created a number of literary types which became the subject of hero-worship. The seventeenth century had had the Courtier, the Gentleman, or in France, the *Honnête Homme*, and finally the Hero. At the turn of the century the Merchant, of English origin, took the lead at a time when the middle class was reaching social pre-eminence and literary repute. The next type was the Scientist: scholars dealing with natural sciences did not retire into their labora-tories or remain in their lecture rooms. Like Maupertuis to the Arctic Circle, Anson to the Antarctic, La Condamine to the Andes, Cook or La Pérouse into the Far South, Saussure up Mont Blanc, they went out into the world. The public was fescinated by their achievements, though they did not always understand them very clearly. Those men travelled far and

14. Two of Commander de Monts de Savasse's statuettes

The head of St John the Baptist, by Pierre Puget

15. Commander Déodat de Dolomieu

Young Maltese woman, by de Favray

wide under very primitive circumstances and sometimes paid with their lives for their discoveries. Hardy travellers never hestitated to wander over land and sea to find a particular shell, a coin or a picture.

Dolomieu was one of these; he was the Naturalist and a romantic figure.

Déodat de Gratet de Dolomieu was born in 1750 in Dolomieu, near La Tour du Pin in Dauphiné. His family was old, of great nobility and little wealth. He had several brothers and sisters, and when he was still a little boy his father had him received into the Order of Malta. There had already been many Dolomieus in the Order, as members of the Langue d'Auvergne. One of his uncles, at that time in Valetta and about to become Commander of Raissac, made things easy for the boy, who received a very sketchy education, since a Knight of Malta was not expected to be a scholar. But he had a keen intelligence which helped him to teach himself many things and to make up for the neglect of his elders. After a short period in school in Paris, he was shipped to Malta at sixteen.

Two years later, while he was sailing on his caravans, he had a quarrel with a colleague in Gaeta; they fought a duel and Dolomieu was unlucky enough to kill his adversary, whose name is unknown. Thus he was faced with a sentence of life imprisonment and the loss of the habit. He was incarcerated in Fort St Elmo, but his friends and relatives did not desert him; they induced the French Prime Minister, Choiseul, and the Pope to put pressure on the Grand Master. Pinto could not refuse Choiseul, the more so because he was trying to ingratiate himself with France at this time. He answered the Minister's letter in the most friendly way and Dolomieu was set free after nine months.[1] It seems that he had accepted his captivity with great composure and never alluded to it later. Colleagues said that during his confinement he had read voraciously and that the nine months of semi-solitude had matured him. When his caravans were done, he made his vows and left for France.

What did the vows of poverty, chastity and obedience mean to him? No more than an undertaking to behave like a gentleman, but he was one of those who could not, anyway, have behaved otherwise. Throughout his life, Dolomieu was an agnostic, to say the least.

Before he set out for Malta he had been for a few months in the French Army, and he returned to it after leaving the island. He was sent to Metz for several years and there he made the acquaintance of Thyrion, a military chemist and anatomist, a very cultured man, with whom he studied biology and natural history. The professor had a daughter, and Dolomieu thought she was even more interesting than her father. She became his mistress and his lifelong friend. He loved her to the end of his life, but was never faithful. She did not mind. Dolomieu also met the Duke Alexandre de la Rochefoucauld d'Enville, a young colonel in the Sarre regiment, and at the same time a philosopher and an amateur scientist who knew many eminent men, including Condorcet and Saussure. He became Dolomieu's intimate friend.

The leading lines of Dolomieu's life were Malta, science, friendship and love, and he pursued them all, constantly broadening his outlook on life. The eighteenth century had no idea of specialization and Dolomieu studied volcanoes, limestone, natural electricity, collected plants, fragments of ore, Greek and Roman coins, books, almost anything. He went back to Malta, where he had to put in an appearance from time to time, to try and get a Commandery. He had nothing to fear now from the duel and his term in prison, and they could not jeopardize his career. After all, Malta was an interesting site for his studies, provided he did not stay too long: there were geological specimens which had never been examined by anybody, and Malta is just about the stoniest island there is!

Dolomieu bought a house with a small garden in the very centre of Valetta, a house which was pompously called a palace, and he took with him his old uncle, spendthrift, debt-ridden and querulous, and he looked after him in a humorous, affectionate way. Their head servant was a devoted Maltese woman, Marguerite, and a fine cook; both uncle and nephew like good cooking. The nephew had stocked his cellar with choice wines: a most necessary precaution in Malta, where the water is undrinkable and scarce. The new Grand Master, Emmanuel de Rohan, had heard that Dolomieu had planted a small and delightful botanical garden, and he was much interested. Dolomieu was in France when he heard of the Grand Master's interest and he offered the garden with the utmost courtesy. In an equally courteous fashion Rohan refused; he did not wish to deprive Dolomieu of it.[2] By that time the young man had left the army for good, and had been elected a corresponding member of the Academy of Sciences. He had also been to Portugal with an Embassy led by the Grand Master's cousin, Prince Camille de Rohan, and he had fallen in love with an English lady, whose name is unknown. He had been given the Commandery of Dolomieu in his home country.

After studying Malta thoroughly, Dolomieu started investigating the geology of southern Italy, Sicily and the little volcanic islands dotted along their coasts. At that time, the English Minister in Naples was William (later Sir William) Hamilton, a clever protector of artists, scientists and travellers. He and his first wife, *née* Barlow, entertained lavishly, either at their palaces in Naples or at their villa at the foot of Mount Pausilippo. William Hamilton was rich, cultured and passionately keen on any intellectual subject. He dabbled in chemistry or natural history, to Dolomieu's amusement, but when he entertained visitors with a taste for music he could play the violin well in a quartet, or sit at his harpsichord and accompany a singer. He took his guests to Capri to bathe, or climbed Vesuvius with a geologist who wanted a close look at an eruption. When in Naples, Dolomieu stayed with him, went with him to Vesuvius or the Campi Phlaegraei, relished his dinners, while admitting that this charming host was completely negligible from a scientific viewpoint.[3]

Starting from Naples with a friend, Commander de Bosredon-Rancijat, Dolomieu explored Sicily. Bosredon drew and Dolomieu made notes. They decided to climb Mount Etna. When they were about to leave the last camp at dead of night, they discovered that their horses had run away. Bosredon flatly refused to make an eleven-hour ascent on foot. Dolomieu was not so squeamish: he was very tall and lean, wiry and immensely strong. So, rousing the guide, who did not like what followed, he slung a bottle of chianti over the man's shoulder and started striding upwards. The guide was disgusted, and soon declared that he was tired, then stopped. Dolomieu shrugged his shoulders, took the bottle and went on alone. He reached the summit, made his observations and came down, perfectly pleased with his expedition. On reaching camp he met Bosredon riding uphill, having caught the horses and brought them back. Dolomieu explained the route and, admitting that he was tired, retired to his tent and fell asleep.' He also visited the Lipari and Aeolian Isles in extremely primitive conditions; he had to sleep on the bare ground, wrapped in his cloak, and eat what he could find, which was not always very appetising.

During his journeys he collected everything and packed his finds into packing cases which he dumped with friends, sent to his sister, the Marquise de Drée, near Grenoble, or shipped to Malta with notes for Marguerite, telling her how to unpack them or how not to unpack them. In the end he was so involved with his collections that he never remembered where any crate in particular was. He sustained heavy losses in Messina at the time of the 1784 earthquake.

All through this frantic life he wrote, made notes, or sent scholarly papers to the Academy of Sciences in Paris. He had an active correspondence with Daubenton, Lacépède, Faujas de St Fond, Horace-Bénédict de Saussure, Sir Joseph Banks, Sir James Hall. Such unquenchable activity would have been more than sufficient for most men, but not for Dolomieu. Back in Malta, he started competing for some of the highest ranks in the hierarchy of the Order. But, in this small island, alive with explosive personalities, rivalries flared up with the utmost violence, and Dolomieu's temper was not a peaceful one. It did not take long for his relations with Rohan to turn out badly. Further, there was a party in Malta intent on helping Naples to grab the island, more or less officially: their leader was Commander de Loras, Dolomieu's enemy. Loras was also party to a plot to bring Russia into the Mediterranean, a scheme which Naples favoured. Malta would have been a convenient base for the Russians. Dolomieu heard of the scheme—possibly through Hamilton, who knew it and opposed it—and he dreaded the results.

When Dolomieu competed for a seat in the Council of the Order, to which he was entitled as Lieutenant of the Marshal of the Order and Governor of Valetta, Loras attacked him furiously, disclosing that Dolomieu had been forbidden to set foot on Neapolitan territories through a decision, without right of appeal, by the King and Queen of Naples. The result was a furious uproar in the Church of St John, at which a young Knight, who was a friend of Dolomieu, d'Andelare, shouted to Loras and his party: 'Here are men who have dishonoured themselves!' A greater uproar followed; d'Andelare was arrested, sentenced to three months' imprisonment and pardoned after an ostentatious application made by Loras himself. Dolomieu was sentenced to house arrest.[5] The Grand Master was much disturbed and rather ashamed of himself: 'Dolomieu, with more common sense and less presumption, would have been a leading light among men at his own level, instead of intriguing and plotting for paltry humbugs,' he wrote to Suffren.[6] Rohan did not like Loras, and felt shy of Dolomieu, who had succeeded in putting himself in a false position.

As soon as his house arrest was over, Dolomieu left Malta, travelled to Rome and initiated legal proceedings against the Order. He was now thirty-seven, loved living dangerously and fully. He settled in Rome and was seen everywhere: he was a delightful guest, a good conversationalist and raconteur, a beautiful dancer and an accomplished horseman. He spent the winter flirting with the Marquise de Pondroit. He sat for Angelica Kauffmann and met Goethe, 'an author very well-known in German for a book that is full of charm and sentiment'. Dolomieu was referring to *Werther*.

All that time Dolomieu was collecting notes about Italian marble, but having no time to visit the quarries; he went to churches instead, making notes on the various marble decorations in Santa Prassede or Santa Maria Maggiore:[7] a rather original approach to geology! His lawsuits continued, in Rome, Aix, Paris and Lyons. He won them but there were endless appeals. He had a powerful enemy in Paris, the Bailly de Suffren, who was Rohan's friend and ambassador. But at the end of 1788 Suffren collapsed and died in his valet's arms of a stroke. Triumph was in sight, thought Dolomieu, but he also wondered what it was really worth in a society the end of which was also near.

For a long time the Commander, like most clear-headed men, had seen the clouds gathering over France. He was in Rome when the Etats-Généraux met. With several of his friends, Bosredon-Rancijat, the Chevalier de Fay, and the Duc de la

Rochefoucauld d'Enville, he favoured new political and social ideas, but was far from being an extremist.

In 1789 Cagliostro arrived in Rome, after having been exiled from France following upon the Affair of the Diamond Necklace. Rome was the last city in the world where he should have set foot. Yet, as in France and Switzerland, he started organizing masonic lodges and among his disciples was—of all people —the Bailly de Loras.[8] An indiscreet letter from Cagliostro was intercepted by the Holy Office: the quack, his wife and several of their disciples were arrested. Loras was still in liberty, but his house had been searched and compromising papers found. The Bailly was in terror; he threw himself upon the mercy of the French Ambassador, the Cardinal de Bernis, and he implored Cardinal Zelada[9] of the Papal Court for help. He was almost continuously in tears and Dolomieu, who had heard the whole story, gloated over it. They met everywhere, as Loras did not dare to hide, since that might have been taken for an admission of guilt. Dolomieu was beside himself with joy, feeling himself revenged. Finally, Loras ran away to Naples, where he hid, waiting for a ship of the Order to enter the harbour; when it did, he slunk on board and retired to Malta, remaining there till the end of his life, cold-shouldered by everybody, including Rohan.

In 1791 Dolomieu went back to France, first to Marseille and afterwards to Paris. One of the first sights he encountered was the procession that carried Voltaire's body to the Pantheon. He had the political situation minutely explained to him: it was extremely dangerous. Among other disquieting items there was talk of confiscating the properties of the Order of Malta. Dolomieu's only income was the rent produced by his Commandery. His youngest brother had now joined the Order and was about to leave to make his caravans and escape from France: Dolomieu offered him his house, and the faithful Marguerite, together with the immortal uncle. The Commander also joined the Club de Feuillants, one of the moderately liberal political societies, and he continued his scientific researches. On October 11, 1791, he wrote to Nicolas-Théodore de Saussure, son of the great naturalist: 'Sir, I owe you many thanks for your interest in the kind of limestone I have brought to the naturalists' attention': this was

the stone that was going to be named *dolomie* by young Saussure, a name that was afterwards given to the mountains of
north-eastern Italy too.[10]

The situation in France continued to darken, and Dolomieu
was disgusted with the violence that boiled up everywhere. He
became acquainted with Narbonne, the War Minister, and
Mme de Staël, his mistress. In October 1792 he wrote to a
friend: 'M. de la Rochefoucauld has been massacred under my
very eyes, almost within my arms. His mother and his wife and
I escaped a similar fate almost by a miracle. I am staying with
this unhappy family to share the danger which still threatens
them.'[11] The tragedy had occurred in Gisors, while the La
Rochefoucauld-d'Envilles, after August 10th, were on their
way to their estate at La Roche-Guyon. The Duke had been
stoned and torn to pieces by the mob. His friend had succeeded
in saving the two women and he remained with them for
several months in order to protect them. A few weeks after the
murder the properties of the Order of Malta in France were
confiscated.

Dolomieu was forty-two and had to begin a new life: he
had lost practically all he possessed, but still must give help to
his old uncle and brother in Malta, and also to his mother and
sisters in Dauphiné. A brother and a sister, Adolphe and
Polyxene, had emigrated. He worked on, even though he was
under sentence of proscription—which meant death if he were
caught. After the end of the Terror, in the summer of 1794,
he showed himself freely in Paris again, and discovered a new,
fascinating object of study: mountains. He was appointed
professor at the School of Mines, and among his duties was the
inspection of the Alpine mines. There were tiny ore lodes near
Servoz and Sixt in Savoy: he visited them and took the opportunity to visit Chamonix and its surroundings. Almost every
year he went to Geneva to meet Saussure, now prematurely
aged after a stroke, very ill, exhausted by his numerous journeys across the Alps. They became great friends and Saussure
always looked forward to meeting this fascinating and charming man. He gave him information and advice on Alpine travel
and Dolomieu was able to make his journeys through the Alps
either on foot or on horseback. In 1794 he wrote: 'My journeys of last summer have left me completely broke.' His horse

had died of exhaustion, a very expensive tragedy, but he had succeeded in climbing the Buet almost without fatigue, and he had been rewarded for this very dull climb by a beautiful view over the mountains.[12]

He now lived for several months each year with his sister de Drée, at La Côte St André, where he was near the Alps. He wrote once: 'In order to get away from the awful aspect of my country in its present situation, I have just visited the glaciers round Mont Blanc and, when I see those majestic mounds, those huge rocks, those eternal snows, I am able for a few moments to forget men's crimes and vile passions.'[13] He went to the Tarentaise, ascended the Allée Blanchée above Courmayeur, crossed the Grand St Bernard, walking for hours at a stretch as tirelessly as when he had climbed Mount Etna. He thought of ascending Mont Blanc, but the weather deteriorated and he could not start.

In Paris, Dolomieu lived in the rue de Seine, in the house of the La Rochefoucauld ladies. He liked teaching, which gave him a means of continuing his researches and giving shape to young minds; he had always liked, and been liked by, young men. It was probably about that time that he met a new and very dear friend, Marie-Jeanne de Maulde, 'kind, sensitive and gay. Ah, Mme de Maulde, why could we not have met when we were both young?' he wrote later! Her maiden name was de Navigheen de Kemmel and she was about thirty-six: he was forty-eight.

A new figure was looming up on the horizon: 'I have often met Bonaparte at the Institut. I never saw anybody with greater control over himself. I do not think one could guess anything he might wish to hide,' Dolomieu wrote. At that time, the great secret scheme was the expedition to Egypt, which he was to disclose a few months later, and Dolomieu was asked to join it as a member of the scientific staff which was to accompany the army. He accepted with great pleasure. Two days before leaving Paris a former pupil, Augustin-Pyrame de Candolle, arrived and called on him: Dolomieu at once suggested that he should go with him to Egypt. Taken aback, the youth demurred and then refused: he had no time to secure his father's permission, and possibly no wish to run so many risks.[14] Dolomieu was sorry, but he took Louis Cordier instead, a handsome youth, full of spirit and courage, one of his favourite pupils. 'I feel towards him like a father,' he was to write, and Cordier was to show himself worthy of this rare affection. On his way through Grenoble, Dolomieu saw Mme de Drée and settled matters with his Genevese friends. One of his last letters from France and addressed to the Genevese scientist Pictet, to let him know that he was shortly to receive a case of geological specimens, brought to him by Jacques Balmat, the Chamonix guide who had made the first ascent of Mont Blanc with Dr Paccard.[15]

Now he was at sea once more, as he had been so often in his youth. The first port of call was Valetta. The insane politics of the German Grand Master, Ferdinand von Hompesch, were on the verge of bringing about what had long been dreaded: Malta becoming a Russian base. This was much too dangerous to be tolerated, and Bonaparte had decided to grab the island before it was too late. Dolomieu was told of the plan when the fleet was about to sail into the Grand Harbour of Valetta. Hompesch resisted for less than two hours; the French Knights had flatly refused to fire on their own countrymen. During the capitulation Dolomieu played a leading part, for he knew everybody in Malta. The other leading character was his friend Bosredon-Rancijat, who was a member of the War Council of the Order. Dolomieu even met Loras, who ran to meet him, completely forgetting the contumely he had piled on his colleague in the past. Dolomieu was full of generosity towards Loras and did all he could to help him.

In Egypt, he threw all his energies into exploring the newly-occupied territory. He was not on very intimate terms with Bonaparte and preferred Kléber, the kind Alsatian giant. He studied old monuments, tried to find a means to protect them from the destructive action of sun and sand, and attempted to work out the date when Pompey's column had been erected. Early in 1799, feeling ill and tired, and longing for a less bohemian sort of life, he got permission to return to France. After so many years, he had decided to go and live with his life-long friend, Mlle Thyrion, who had always adored him.

He sailed with General Dumas (Alexandre Dumas' father) and his dear pupil, Louis Cordier. Their ship, badly battered by a storm, had to take shelter in Taranto; the passengers were arrested as prisoners-of-war and taken captive to Messina, where they were imprisoned for two months. It was discovered that one of them was the Commander de Dolomieu; he was separated from his companions, robbed of everything he had, and thrown into a disgusting cell, without light and almost without air, and in stifling heat, where he passed twenty-one months.

He had been left, or had managed to hide, a few books. He succeeded in making pencils from splinters of wood burnt brown over his candle, and he started to write on the blank pages, in the margins or between the lines.[18] He wrote anything which came into his head, merely to while away the endless hours and to save his reason. He had no hope of ever emerging from his living tomb.

Dolomieu, who hitherto had written nothing but scientific articles, showed himself almost a poet when he tried to charm away his misery and boredom. His writing is simple and quiet, yet beautifully sensitive. He wrote down his thoughts as they occurred to him. In sentences like: 'If only I could be switched out quickly like my lamp! To exist in this way is not to live!' one hears the true ring of despair. He went on to list all he had lost, his freedom, the sight of the world, of the sea, of the mountains, of the sky, of the great phenomena of Nature, his country, his friends, and the affections with which he had always been surrounded. 'Now,' he went on, 'I have no shelter against boredom; it never leaves me, it is beside me, in front of me, behind me, I breathe it in the air, I eat it, drink it; it creeps to the marrow of my bones, I cannot even find a remedy against it in its excess, which usually brings sleep, as I hardly ever sleep a wink. Obviously, boredom does not kill, as I am still alive.'

Such is the melancholy burden of his long meditation. He had given up hope; he was only asking for dignity and resignation, 'the dignity of La Rochefoucauld, slaughtered almost within my arms, the fortitude of Bailly during the contumely and torments which he endured before his execution, the courage of so many illustrious victims, murdered by the most atrocious tyranny, the resignation and bravery of a so-called weaker sex at the moment of final sacrifice: the calm of all those who went to the scaffold innocent of crime. . . .' He went

back in thought to the woman who had loved him for so long:
'You wait for me, my dear friend! God knows how long you
are likely to wait, and He alone knows if you are waiting in
vain. . . . And I too am waiting; I wait furiously for the end of
each day, each week, each month. . . . Because each passing
moment is a conquest of the future. But how slow the future is
in coming! Days have for me as many hours as they have
minutes for others, and who can reckon how endlessly long
are my nights? . . .'

He wrote everything that came into his mind, simply in
order to stop thinking. He made his will, to be delivered to
Mme de Drée.[17] He drew up a list of his friends, in Paris, at
home, in Geneva, in England. He wrote pen-portraits of some
of them. They are short, pithy, witty and kind, and evince a
quiet courage, when one thinks of the conditions under which
they were written.

Many tried to help him. Cordier had succeeded in getting
back to France, and with all his energy he clamoured for help
for his beloved professor. Public opinion was at first surprised
and afterwards indignant. Why was this great scholar sub-
jected to such protracted torture? Because, years ago, his discovery of the Russian intrigue had brought him the hatred of
Queen Maria-Carolina of Naples. The Institut officially lodged
an appeal with the Directoire. The Minister of Foreign Affairs,
Reinhard, sent out a diplomatic note, explaining Dolomieu's
fate, appealing to the world's conscience. Another attempt was
made by Sir Joseph Banks, President of the Royal Society; he
was a friend of Dolomieu, and in spite of the war he acted at
once, inducing Sir William Hamilton, who was back in Naples,
to act too. Lady Hamilton was the Queen of Naples's friend, as
well as Nelson's mistress. Hamilton worked energetically on
Dolomieu's behalf; he made his wife and Nelson write to the
Queen, but it was all of no avail. Charles IV of Spain was
brought into the campaign. But the only result was that Acton,
Prime Minister of Naples, promised that Dolomieu would not
be delivered to the Czar Paul I, who had been declared Protector of the Order of Malta by Hompesch, then illegal Grand
Master who was claiming Dolomieu as his captive, to have him
tortured and put to death. But the unhappy man's fate was not
made lighter.

Then Bonaparte triumphed at Marengo, the coalition collapsed and the First Consul made Dolomieu's liberation a main article of the peace treaty with Naples. A few days later Dolomieu was freed, and he thanked the Institut from Florence, where he was resting.

He was enthusiastically received in Paris by his friends and colleagues. From Nancy, Mlle Thyrion wrote gaily, organizing her removel to Paris to live with her lover, but warning him against too great fatigue: 'My beloved friend, I see in the papers that, since you came back you have been constantly going from feast to feast and show to show: I am greatly disturbed. Remember the unhappy fate of Vert-Vert the parrot.[18] To avoid this and calm my anxiety, in God's name, do not eat too many sweets!'

Dolomieu began a series of lectures on science at the Museum and, as the summer had come, he rushed to the Alps to see his beloved mountains once more. Together with a Danish scientist, Bruun-Neergaard, he crossed almost the whole of the Alps, travelling as far as Tessin and the Grisons. He had taken Jacques Balmat as his guide and he climbed a few summits near the Grand St Bernard. In Brig he met the Italian physicist Volta. Saussure had been dead for two years, but most of the other Geneva scientists were his friends and welcomed him warmly. 'The great Dolomieu . . . is here,' wrote Mme Gosse, one of his Genevese friends. 'Yet he has forgotten all his sufferings to enjoy his freedom and his friends. To the greatest scholarly gift he adds modesty, simplicity and sweetness: a most charming temper altogether. He is over fifty, has suffered much and yet enjoys the strength of youth and the gaiety which goes with it.' He was admired, worshipped, petted and spoilt, and he went back to his sister's chateau delighted with his summer, ready to plan a new journey and about to go back to Paris to meet his mistress.

He never saw her again. He was taken ill suddenly and died in a week in the arms of his sister and brother-in-law. A few days later, M. de Drée wrote to Cordier: 'Dolomieu, whom you loved as much as I did, to whom you proved so devoted and affectionate, and whom you helped to rescue from captivity, has just ended his days in our arms, on the eighth day of an infectious fever.'[19]

CONCLUSION

WHEN the active life of the Order ended with Bonaparte's landing in Malta in 1798, the Order had already become obsolete. It no longer had any function to perform and its medieval framework had already been split by the powerful and unruly personalities of its members. For the Knights I have portrayed in this book are not exceptions, with the rest merely conventional characters; they have been selected from a very long list. Few of them are well known and most of them had to be rediscovered in practically unexplored archives; but the figures which emerge from the dust that covers these old papers are striking enough.

There were many fiery young men: the Verdelin brothers,[1] for instance, one of who aided his brother's escape from Fort St Elmo, where he had been confined for life after a duel; both were eventually pardoned and in due time reached the rank of Commander. There was also Commander de Bonnifas, a descendant of the notorious Joseph de Bonnifas de la Molle, Queen Margot's lover; he used to visit his Commandery of Tirlemont accompanied by his Maltese mistress.[2] Two Ambassadors to the Court of France, the Commander de Souvré and the Bailly de Mesmes, led extremely colourful lives. The former was one of the noted *gourmets* at Court and had founded an exclusive dining club; he was a man of taste and courage and a good diplomat. The latter, one of Saint-Simon's pet aversions, also proved to be a clever diplomat, though the Court was hugely amused when his mistress, the lovely ballerina Mlle Prévost, sued him in order to compel him to continue paying her pension, though she had married his rival.

A Knight of Malta, the Chevalier de Ganges, murdered his beautiful sister-in-law and was subsequently refused asylum in Malta: this was one of the outstanding seventeenth-century *crimes passionnels*.[3] In a much more sedate line, it was a Knight of Malta who was one of the witnesses of the first ascent of Mont Blanc in August 1786: Meyer de Knonau, a Frenchman of Swiss origin. Many more outstanding men can be quoted. The Bailly de Mirabeau, a powerful, intelligent and kind man, stood out as a tower of strength.[4] Joseph de Fassion de Sainte-Jay was a humorous writer and great book collector.

Gaspard de la Croix de Sayve was a good geologist who corresponded with Horace-Bénédict de Saussure. A list of the striking characters among the Knights would be very long, but after this attempt to bring a few of them back to life, one discovers that certain aspects of the period in which they lived have become more tangible.

The seventeenth century emerges as more colourful and more heroic than one might expect. The great baroque ideals gave a vivid light to the Knights' adventures. They led a realistic life in a fairy-tale setting: such was the case of Tourville during the Maltese period of his life, Téméricourt, Königsmark, Dubois de la Ferté, the captives in Algiers. They attempted to tune their lives to a religious or heroic harmony. Their faith and their honour, on the same level, were the two things they thought worth fighting for, and when either was in danger they did not flinch from possible death. A short time ago, under almost similar circumstances, Commandant Denois de Saint Mars remarked: 'You can ask a soldier to die, that is his job; but not to lie and perjure himself.'[5] That might have been the motto of those seventeenth-century Knights. They had an ideal, though it was not always a religious one. The members of the Order were staunch individualists and hardly ever accepted any restraint.

During the eighteenth century more unexpected trends developed among them. They were scarcely ever interested in religious problems, and some of them were complete agnostics, but they succeeded in keeping their dignity. A curious aspect of the moral attitude of the Order is underlined in the great conventual church of St John in Valetta. The whole floor is made of tombstones wrought in coloured marble mosaic. It looks like a huge and gorgeous carpet, most impressive in its shiny brilliance. Each tombstone bears the Knight's epitaph, his coat-of-arms, and some allegory—Time, Destiny, Fame, Hercules. Some tombstones are decorated with drawings of Greek vases, a cemetery, a vault, a small seascape seen through a kind of porthole, sea fights during which the dead Knight achieved some glorious deed. An impressive death dance weaves its way across the church: it was done long before the time when Young in his *Night Thoughts* made graves fashionable, so to speak. Skeletons pray, meditate, wrap themselves in winding sheets, blow trumpets, ride clocks, destroy busts, carry coffins, or just recline in death. All over the church they seem to repeat: *'Odie mihi, cras tibi!'* Fat little cherubs hover over them, play with them and lend some gaiety to the grim heralds of mortality. The strange feature about all this striking decoration is the total absence of religious symbol: there is just one tomb on which a cross appears, clasped by a veiled woman; otherwise the only cross is the eight-pointed one, against which stand all the coats-of-arms. In this it is difficult to decide whether pride or humility is implied: possibly the latter. In heraldry, a coat-of-arms stands for the man himself: thus it is offered in homage to God and a Knight could not offer more. Yet, it is strange that the symbolism throughout the church is stoic, or almost pagan, possibly displaying a lofty indifference to death and the hereafter.

All this, nevertheless, is quite in keeping with eighteenth-century ideals, for by then religion had lost most, if not all, of its appeal and the Knights lived according to a purely secular conception of life, being served by the Order instead of serving it. After all, why not? Its mission had now been fulfilled and it had turned to helping men who had actually made some sacrifice to come to Malta and take their vows.

Most of the eighteenth-century Knights stand out as active, restless, often tormented men who tried, not always successfully, to lead modern lives within the antiquated framework of the island fortress. Malta never was a peaceful place and had become a real hornet's nest by the end of the eighteenth century. After the fall of the island the Order led a vagrant life, drifted to Russia, where it was welcomed with open arms by Paul I (who was hoping to be able to grab the island at last), and was then practically kicked out of the country when the hope of seizing Malta vanished with its occupation by Nelson in 1801. That was the end, if not of the Order yet of the picturesque, independent, proud life it had lived from the time of its creation in the Holy Land.

*　　*　　*

It is almost impossible to know for certain what its strength had been. There are no statistics, and there is not even a list of the Knights who died in Valetta, apart from the names of those who died in the hospitals of the Order. What follows is therefore a rather uncertain attempt to reach a figure. In 1778, according to a list published in Valetta of Knights belonging to the three French langues, there were 356 Knights of Provence, 91 of Auvergne, and 560 of France. As it seems that the three French tongues accounted for the two-thirds of the Order, roughly, the whole strength might have been something round 1,500 Knights.

When Bonaparte landed in Malta, the Order had no more than five or six serviceable ships, and its fleet had never been powerful so far as numbers went. It never counted more than ten or twelve sailing ships and galleys, with small units in addition; but there were other ships privately owned by Knights who fought as corsairs under the Order's flag. Its navy was the Order's best contribution to the defence of Western Europe.

In 1681, M. de Viviers, a captain in the French Royal Navy, was commissioned to draw up a report on the galleys of Malta, which he had met when fighting in Crete.[6] He was a great friend of the Chevalier d'Escrainville, who had fought under Téméricourt a few years earlier; thus he had spent three days on board his friend's ship, *La Madeleine*, and collected all the required data. The Maltese galleys were among the best of their kind, but there were only seven of them. They were strong and well equipped, and their crews were well fed and cared for. The officers were not so good, for they were changed too often, and the real leaders were the NCOs, who had permanent appointments. Their sailors were much better than the Turks, who were poor sailors on the whole. The Grand Master—Caraffa at that time—knew much about ships and supervised them closely. Captains were usually twenty-five years old and some of them were even younger. The crews totalled about 420 men, including 300 rowers, of whom 200 were slaves. Wounded or sick sailors were well looked after in the Order's hospitals. But Viviers was not at all complimentary about the young Knights, 'who spend their time gambling when at sea and sight-seeing when ashore'. Yet they fought well.

Periodically ships were neglected and a serious accident

(like the sinking of a galley in 1700) reminded Grand Masters that the situation should be examined more closely and obsolete craft scrapped and replaced. At the beginning of the eighteenth century most galleys had to be taken out of commission, and some were replaced by sailing ships; but new galleys were built, for they were light and useful in Mediterranean conditions.

When the Order left the island in 1798, it had outlived its mission. Its members could no longer perform a task worthy of their rank, their traditions and their past. They had lost touch with the facts of a quickly changing life. Rohan's *Code*, published in 1787, was already an anachronism, coming nine years after the *Declaration of Independence* and two years before the *Rights of Man*. Yet, during the two centuries and a half it had remained in Malta, the Order had succeeded in bringing out a large number of outstanding and sometimes eccentric men who could not have emerged from any other setting.

NOTES

CHAPTER I
1 Royal Library of Malta: *Testaments*
2 Vatican Library. Malta 132. No date, but the letter of the Inquisitor, which accompanied the Minister's letter, is dated August 15, 1768

CHAPTER II
1 Jean de Beaugué: *Histoire de la guerre d'Ecosse*
2 ibid
3 *High Treasury of Scotland*, T.IX, 1546
4 Bibliothèque Nationale. Duc d'Aumale: *Correspondence* (Ecosse). MSS Français, 20457
5 Ibid
6 *Calendar of State Papers*, Scotland, 1547-52
7 *Opera*. Letters, July 6, 1560

CHAPTER III
1 Royal Library of Malta. Langue de France—Arch. 2112

CHAPTER IV
1 Royal Library of Malta. *Liber Conciliorum*, August 5, 1662, Arch. 122
2 Des Barres: *Etat présent de la Morée*
3 *Mémoires*, 1753
4 La Magdelaine, *Le miroir ottoman*, 1677
5 *Journal d'un voyage en Perse*, 1686
6 Mme de Staël-Holstein's husband was a great-grand nephew of the Chevalier. Pierre-Robert de Staël was received into the Langue d'Allemagne on July 11, 1664 (*Liber Conciliorum*, Arch. 122)
7 Public Record Office, SP 86/11. August 15, 1678

CHAPTER V
1 Apparently, Madame, the Palatine Princess, met the Countess of Southampton

CHAPTER VI
1 Order of St John's headquarters; Library and Museum of St John's Gate, Clerkenwell
2 It was the campaign during which Königsmark died

CHAPTER VII

1 Vatican Library, Malta 51. Bishop Ascanio Bentivoglio wrote on March 6, 1700
2 Vuillari. Letters to Préfontaine. See also Marquis de Sourches, *Mémoires*, T.VI, April 19, 1700
3 Sourches, ibid
4 Archives Nationales, Consuls B7 Marine 26, June 1, 1715
5 Archives Nationales, Consuls B7 Marine 26, June 7, 1715
6 Ibid, June 18, 1715
7 Ibid, July 1715

CHAPTER VIII

1 Royal Library of Malta. Arch. 1216
2 They were Maltese soldiers and not knights. The Knights were not the Grand Master's subjects
3 Now called the Château Neuf
4 Royal Library of Malta. Arch. 1229
5 Ibid, June 25, 1708
6 Ibid
7 Ibid
8 Ibid, December 6, 1708
9 Cromelin, *Voyage pour la rédemption des captifs, fait en 1720*. The story of the enslaved Knights was still well remembered at that time, but Cromelin's version gives a much too active and compassionate part to the monks: he belonged to their Order
10 Royal Library of Malta. Arch. 1229
11 Ibid
12 Ibid
13 Arch. 1561
14 Arch. 1228
15 Arch. 1218
16 Arch. 1228
17 Archives Nationales, Consuls B7 Marine 25. Letter from the Chevalier de Montmorency-Laval. December 12, 1714
18 Ibid, B7 Marine 26. Letter from the Grand Master, March 30, 1715
19 Royal Library of Malta. Arch. 1218
20 Ibid
21 Ibid, July 30, 1715
22 Ibid
23 Rhône Archives (Lyons). Letter from Commander de Monts de Savasse. April 14, 1765

24 Rhône Archives. Letter from Commander de Monts de Savasse. November 1765
25 Royal Library of Malta. Arch. 1204. June 18, 1765

CHAPTER IX
1 Royal Library of Malta. Arch. 1202
2 Ibid, Arch. 3360
3 Ibid, Arch 1218
4 Ibid, Arch. 1563
5 Rhône Archives (Lyons). April 24, 1765
6 Royal Library of Malta. Arch. 1223
7 Vatican Library, Malta 131
8 Archives Nationales, M. 999. The English envoy who called on the Bailly was Robert Walpole, the writer's cousin

CHAPTER X
1 Letter to Jennings, March 30, 1713; letter to Queen Anne, March 1713. Both are in the Royal Library of Malta. Arch. 1561
2 Ibid, Arch. 1217. June 13, 1713
3 Ibid, October 18, 1713
4 Ibid, January 22, 1714
5 Quoted by La Varende in *Tourville*
6 Archives Nationales, Consul, B7 Marine 26. Letter from the Chevalier de Cominges, April 4, 1715
7 Ibid, B7 Marine 40. December 12, 1719
8 Royal Library of Malta. *Liber Conciliorum*. Arch. 267, April 20, 1722. A long report covering the whole of Montmorency-Laval's journeys abroad
9 Archives Nationales. M. 953
10 Public Record Office, SP 86/1. February 8, 1720
11 Ibid, January 24, 1720
12 Ibid, SP 86/2
13 Ibid, SP 86/1. March 8, 1720
14 Public Record Office, SP 103/36
15 Montmorency-Laval's report. Arch. 267. *Liber Conciliorum*
16 Royal Library of Malta. Arch. 57
17 Polworth Papers. Edinburgh-HMC T, II
18 Royal Library of Malta. Arch. 57. June 10, 1720

CHAPTER XI
1 Public Record Office, 78/151, 1687-88
2 H. A. Le Fleming, MSS HMC 1890. December 15, 1688

3 Public Record Office, SP 86/1, December 15, 1687
4 Ibid, December 9, 1687
5 Royal Library of Malta. *Liber Conciliorum*. December 8, 1687. Arch. 263
6 Ibid, *Liber Epistolarum*. July 13, 1689. Arch. 57
7 Ibid, Arch. 1566
8 Ibid, Arch. 1262
9 Ibid, Arch. 1205
10 Ibid, Registres de la Langue de France. Arch. 2119
11 Ibid, Arch. 1582. See also Archives Nationales, M. 961

CHAPTER XII

1 F. Roux-Devillas Collection
2 Comte Jean de Bonneval's family archives
3 April 11, 1714
4 Quoted by Courteaulx in his book. The MSS belongs to the Bonneval family
5 *Correspondence*
6 Quoted by Courteaulx. The MSS belongs to the Bonneval family
7 Quoted by Asse in the Appendix of his edition of the spurious *Lettres*
8 Family tradition
9 Lettre to d'Argental, August 5, 1734, belonging to Dr Lafon, unpublished. The copy of the letter had been given to me by M. Jean de Beaugourdon
10 Letter to Froullay
11 Ibid
12 Ibid

CHAPTER XIII

1 Archivio del Stato, Verona
2 Bailly Le Cœur to Froullay, August 3, 1750. Archives Nationales, M. 954
3 Bibliothèque Nationale, MSS Français, 5104. Letters from the Embassy in Constantinople
4 Upsala University, MSS Ihre 192
5 Ibid, MSS Bosse 36
6 Ibid
7 MSS Dupan—Freudenreich, Bibliothèque Publique et Universitaire, Geneva
8 Royal Library of Malta. Arch. 1234. September 22 and October 10, 1751

9 Archives Nationales, M. 989
10 Bodleian Library, MSS Dob. c 56, ff 45-6
11 Ibid, April 19, 1773
12 Ibid, January 29, 1774
13 Royal Library of Malta. Arch. 6106

CHAPTER XIV
1 Rhône Archives (Lyons), H. 43, Pièce No. 2
2 Quoted by J. de la Harpe, *J. P. de Crousaz*
3 Archivio del Stato, Venice. Professor Halsband, presently editing Lady Mary's correspondence, discovered this letter in Venice, very kindly showed me the text and allowed me to mention it.
4 Ibid
5 Ibid
6 Pinto to the Ambassador in Paris. Archives Nationales, M. 955. July 3, 1757

CHAPTER XV
1 Fribourg Archives. Griset de Forel, Correspondence, February 2, 1722
2 August 31, 1722
3 February 26, 1737
4 January 15, 1735
5 1736
6 1736
7 Ibid
8 Ibid
9 October 28, 1736
10 January 8, 1737
11 January 16, 1737
12 April 28, 1737
13 April 28, 1737
14 June 19, 1737
15 December 20, 1737
16 April 17, 1738
17 August 25, 1739
18 October 30, 1743
19 May 12, 1758

CHAPTER XVI
1 Gonzague de Monts de Savasse's private archives. April 1, 1731
2 Ibid

3 Ibid
4 Ibid
5 St Fonds to President Dugas, *Correspondence Littéraire et anecdotique*. August 11, 1735
6 Gonzague de Monts de Savasse's archives. July 9, 1766, and August 11, 1765
7 Rhône Archives, H. 48, p. 1,978. Pièces diverses 42-74
8 Gonzague de Monts de Savasse's archives. December 27, 1755
9 Ibid, February 24, 1766
10 Ibid, February 27, 1766
11 Ibid, February 27, 1766
12 The Princess, who was hardly more than a child, eloped with her very young husband, as they had been separated again after the ceremony and she had been sent back to her convent. In spite of such a romantic beginning, the marriage proved a failure
13 Gonzague de Monts de Savasses's archives. February 22, 1766
14 Ibid, March 15, 1767
16 Archives Nationales, M. 945. See also a letter in the Rhône Archives, July 6, 1768

CHAPTER XVII
1 Royal Library of Malta. Arch. 1235. The *speronare* was a swift rowing boat, used when there was an urgent message to carry
2 Ibid, Arch. 1235. February 15, 1753
3 Ibid
4 Vatican Library, Malta 131. June 22, 1659
5 Ibid
6 Public Record Office, SP 93/24. July 10, 1769
7 Royal Library of Malta. Arch. 1237
8 Ibid, Arch. 1238
9 Ibid, Arch. 1238. January 31, 1775
10 Ibid
11 Archives Nationales, MM. 1045

CHAPTER XVIII
1 Roland de la Platière, *Lettres écrites de Suisse . . . et de Malte*. He describes the theatre and the company a short time before des Adrets came to Malta
2 Vatican Library, Malta 144
3 Ibid, June 2, 1688
4 Ibid

5 Royal Library of Malta. Arch. 1536. August 2, 1788
6 A necklace he gave her, studded with golden eight-pointed crosses, is in the museum of St John's Gate, Clerkenwell. She died long after him and was buried in his tomb in St John, Valetta, the only woman to be buried in the Knights' Conventual Church
7 Royal Library of Malta. Arch. 1538. October 2, 1788
8 Ibid, November 8, 1788
9 Ibid
10 Ibid, Arch. 1622
11 Ibid, Arch. 1538. February 21, 1789
12 Ibid

CHAPTER XIX
1 The portrait belongs to Mrs Cassar-Torregiani (Sliema, Malta)
2 In the sacristy of St John, Valetta
3 Baron Meurgey de Tupigny's collection, Paris
4 National Museum, Valetta
5 Ibid
6 Mr Debono's collection, Rabat, Malta
7 In the Louvre
8 Archives Nationales, MM. 1040
9 It belonged to the Comte de Vergennes and was stolen from his chateau during the last war
10 Museum of Marseille
11 Museum of Toulouse
12 Comte de Vergenne's collection
13 Royal Library of Malta. Boyer's diary, Libr. 137
14 Quoted by Léon Boppe, *Les Peintres du Bosphore*
15 National Gallery of Scotland, Edinburgh

CHAPTER XX
1 Lacroix. *Dolomieu's Letters*, 1769
2 Ibid, April 13, 1782
3 Ibid, Ch. Duclos (*Voyage en Italie*, 1806) was in Naples in 1766. Hamilton took him up Vesuvius: it was the Ambassador's twenty-second ascent of the mountain. Duclos goes on: 'Mr and Mrs Hamilton are the happiest couple I ever met. They are both still young, with upright hearts, cultured minds and the same tastes, and they love each other in a way which made me understand what patriarchal life is.' She was the Ambassador's first wife

4 Abbé de St Non, *Voyage pittoresque de Naples et de Sicile*
5 Royal Library of Malta. Arch. 1622
6 Ibid, June 28, 1687
7 His notes are in the archives of the Académie des Sciences in Paris
8 Lacroix, *Lettres*
9 Royal Library of Malta. Arch. 1241
10 Bibliothèque Publique et Universitaire, Geneva. Saussure's papers. Dossier K. October 30, 1781
11 Lacroix, *Lettres*. October 4, 1782
12 Ibid, October 13, 1784
13 Ibid, September 7, 1795
14 M. R. de Candolle's archives, Geneva, February 19, 1796
15 To Pictet, on board the *Tonnant*, May 20, 1798. Lacroix, *Lettres*
16 Museum d'Histoire Naturelle, Paris
17 Ibid. One of the books was Fanjas de Saint-Fond's treatise on volcanoes
18 Lacroix, *Lettres*. The parrot Vert-Vert is the hero of a mock heroic poem by Gresst, *Vert-Vert* (1734)
19 Lacroix, *Lettres*

CONCLUSION

1 Vatican Archives, Malta 65. December 1717
2 Royal Library of Malta. Arch. 1582. 1777
3 Saint-Simon, *Mémoires*; also Archives Nationales, M. 986-1658
4 Loménie (L. de), *Les Mirabeau*, Prais. 5 vols. 1879
5 At his trial in Paris, June 1961
6 Archives Nationales, B7 Marine, 509

BIBLIOGRAPHY

I MSS SOURCES

A *Royal Library of Malta*
Letters from the Grand Masters
Letters to the Grand Masters
Lettres de la Cour
Lettres des Ambassadeurs
Langue de France
Langue d'Auvergne
Libri Conciliorum
Libri Epistolarum
Spoglie
Hôpital
Testaments
Suppliche
Giornale di Viaggi
Commander de Chambray: *Mémoires*
Chevalier de Cuny: *Réflexions d'un chevalier de Malte*
Abbé Boyer: *Lettres et mémoires*

B *Vatican Library*
Malta

C *Archives Nationales*
Fonds de l'Ambassade de Malte
Lettres et Correspondence des Ambassadeurs
Consuls (B7 Marine)

D *Bibliothèque Nationale*
Cabinet des Titres
MSS Français
Duc d'Aumale: *Correspondence Ecosse*
Lettres de l'Ambassadeur à Constantinople

E *Academie des Sciences*
Dolomieu's papers and notes

F *Rhône Archives (Lyons)*
Monts de Savasse's papers

G *Muséum (Paris)*
Dolomieu's will

H *Public Record Office*
Letters from Malta, SP 86/1 to 86/4
Letters from Naples, SP 91/24 to 91/30

I *British Museum*
G. Wood: *Journal of a Voyage in the Mediterranean,* Add MSS
 19306
G. Halestyn: *A Journal kept of a straight Voyage,* Sloane MSS
 2755
Sir William Hamilton, Correspondence, Egerton MSS 2635
R. Payne-Knight, catalogue of his collection

J *St John's Gate, Clerkenwell*
Various Letters

K *Edinburgh Register House*
Lord Polworth Papers

L *State Archives of Fribourg*
Francis de Griset de Forel: Letters

M *Archivio del Stato, Verona*
Commenda di S. Vitale e Sepolcro—Registro della Visita del
 miglioranti, 1774
Antiche estimi, Vol. 17. cc 646
Sagramoso's Correspondence

N *University of Upsala*
MSS letters to Dr J. Ihre. MSS Ihre, 192
MSS letters to H. A. Gyllenborg, MSS Posse, 36

O *Bibliothèque Publique et Universitaire—Geneva*
Saussure's Pappers
Dupon de Freudenreich: *Correspondance*

P *Private Archives*
Comte Gonzague de Monts de Savasse
Comte du Corail (La Richardie)
M. Roger de Candolle (Dolomieu)
M. F. Roux-Devillas (Mlle Aïssé)
Serrapiccola Archives (at the State Archives of Naples)—
 Sagromoso

II PRINTED SOURCES

Anderson: *General Naval Wars,* London, 1965
Cavaliero: *The Last Crusaders,* London, 1960
Boisgelin, L. de: *Malta Ancient and Modern,* 2 vols., London 1804
Dangeau, Marquis de: *Journal,* 19 vols., Paris, 1860
Doucet: *Mémoires Historiques,* ed. Panisse-Passis, Paris, 1883
Engel, C. E.: *L'Ordre de Malte en Méditerranée,* Paris, 1953; *Le
 Veritable Abbé Prévost,* Paris, 1954; *Les Chevaliers de Malte,*
 Paris, 1961

Eves, C. K.: *Matthew Prior*, New York, 1940
Godechot, J.: *Histoire de Malte*, Paris 1952
Hazard, P.: *La crise de la Conscience Européenne*, 3 vols., Paris, 1936; *La Conscience Européenne au XVIIIe siècle*, 3 vols., Paris, 1948
King, E. J.: *The Knights of St John in the British Empire*, London, 1934
La Roncière, J. de: *Histoire de la Marine Française*, 6 vols., Paris, 1932
Legge, N.: *Matthew Prior*, London, 1921
Luke, Sir H.: *Malta*, London, 1949
Luynes, Duc de: *Mémoires*, 15 vols., Paris, 1886
Mas-Latrie, M. L. de: *Archives, bibliothèque et inscriptions de Malte*, Paris, 1865
Michel de Pierredon, Cte: *Histoire de l'Ordre Souverain de Malte*, Paris, 1956
Miège, M.: *Histoire de Malte*, 3 vols., Paris, 1840
Rossi, E.: *Storia della Marina del 'Ordine di Malta*, Rome, 1926
Ryan, F. W.: *The House of the Temple*, London, 1931
Saint-Simon, Duc de: *Mémoires*, ed. Boislisle, 42 vols., Paris
Savelli, A.: *Storia di Malta*, Milan, 1943
Scicluna, Sir H.: *The Church of St John in Malta*, Rome, 1956
Sourches, Marquis de: *Mémoires*, 14 vols., Paris, 1883
Vertot, Abbé de: *Histoire des chevaliers de Malte*, 7 vols., Paris, 1770
Viviani, L.: *Storia du Malta*, Turin, 1934

CHAPTER I

Beaumont and Fletcher: *The Knight of Malta*
Brantôme: *Oeuvres*, ed. Lalanne, 11 vols.
Hughes, Q.: *The Building of Malta*, London, 1958
Massinger: *The Maid of Honour*
Saint-Allais: *Nobiliaire Universel de France*, 21 vols., Paris, 1875
Taylor, R.: *Charles V*, London, 1956
Voltaire: *Correspondence*, ed. Besterman, Geneva
Winterfeld: *Die Johanniter*, Berlin

CHAPTER II

Beaugué, J. de: *Histoire de la guerre d'Ecosse*, Bordeaux, 1862
Calvin, J.: *Opera (Epistolae)*
Lehr, A.: *Protestants d'autrefois sur terre et sur mer*, Paris, 1907
Léry, J. de: *La France Antarctique*
Maimbourg: *Histoire du Calvinisme*, Paris, 1652.

Marie de Lorraine: *Foreign Correspondence*, Edinburgh, 3 vols., 1923-27

CHAPTER III

Farrère, C.: *Une Aventure amoureuse de M. de Tourville*, Paris, 1925
Jal, A.: *Abraham Duquesne*, Paris, 1873
La Varende, J. de: *Tourville et son temps*, Paris, 1843
Magron, Abbé de: *Mémoires de M. de Tourville*, 3 vols., Paris, 1758

CHAPTER IV

Arvieux Chevalier d': *Mémoires*, 6 vols., Paris, 1735
Brémond d'Ars, A. de: *Le chevalier de Téméricourt, un martyr oublié*, Paris, 1904
Chardin, Sir John: *Journal de voyage en Perse*, London, 1686
Des Barres: *Etat présent de l'Archipel*, Cologne, 1678
Engel, C. E.: 'Un chevalier de Malte Protestant: Le chevalier de Téméricourt', *Bulletin de la Societé d'Histoire du Protestantisme Française*, 1959
La Magdelaine, L. C. de: *Le Miroir Ottoman*, Bâle, 1672
Randolph, B.: *The Present State of the Morea*, London, 1689
Vandal, A.: *Voyages du Marquis de Nointel*, Paris, 1900
Villeneuve-Bargemont: *Monuments des Grands Maîtres de Malte*, 2 vols., Paris, 1899

CHAPTER V

Aulnoy, M. de: *Relation du Voyage d'Espagne*, La Haye, 1705
Beckman, V. A.: *Aurora Königsmark och hennes Bröder*, Stockholm, 1948
Blaze de Bury: 'Mlle de Königsmark', *Revue des Deux Mondes*, 1882
Evelyn, J.: *Diary*, ed. E. S. de Beer, 6 vols., Oxford, 1956
Godley, E.: *The Trial of Count Königsmark*, London, 1929
Reresby, Sir John: *Memoirs*
Orleans, Duchess of: *Correspondance*, 3 vols.

CHAPTER VI

Grandet, J.: *La vie de Messire Gabriel Dubois de la Ferté*, Paris, 1712

CHAPTER VII

Acton, H.: *The Last Medici*, London, 1932

Caylus, Comte de: *Voyage d'Italie*, ed. A. Pons, Paris, 1914
Vuillard, G.: *Lettres à L. de Préfontaine*, ed. R. Clark, Geneva, 1950

CHAPTER VIII

Artefeuille, d': *Histoire héroïque de la noblesse de Provence*, Avignon
Cromelin, P.: *Voyage pour la rédemption des Captifs fait en 1720*, Paris, 1721

CHAPTER IX

Marais, M.: *Journal et mémoires*, 4 vols., Paris, 1863

CHAPTER X

Byng, P.: *Journal, 1718-1720*, ed. Comm. Byng, Navy Record Society, 1950
Engel, C. E.: 'Les Aventures de M. de Bonneval', *Carrefours de l'histoire*, 1962
La Varende, J. de: *Tourville et son temps*, Paris, 1943
Vandal, A.: *La Pacha de Bonneval*, Paris, 1885
François de Montmorency-Laval, 1er évéque de Québec, Montreal, 1871

CHAPTER XI

Dyer, T. E.: *Admiral Sir John Narbrough*
Lart, C. E.: *Jacobite extracts from the Parochial Registers of St Germain-en Laye*, 2 vols., London, 1910
Teonge, H.: *Diary*, London, 1827

CHAPTER XII

Aïssé, Mlle: *Lettres*, ed. Asse, Paris, 1875
Andrieux, M.: *Mlle Aïssé*, Paris, 1952
Aydie, Chevalier d': *Correspondance*, Paris, 1874
Bolingbroke, Viscount: *Correspondance*, 3 vols., Paris, 1808; *Works and Letters*, 7 vols., London, 1775
Ballara, C.: *The Great Earl of Peterborough*, London, 1929
Courteaulx, A.: *Mlle Aïssé, le chevalier d'Aydie et leur fille*, Paris, 1908
Dussolier, E.: *Le chevalier d'Aydie et Mlle Aïssé*, Périgueux, 1924
Engel, C. E.: 'Voltaire et Mlle Aïssé', *Revue des Deux Mondes*, 1952; 'Les Lettres de Mlle Aïssé', ibid, 1961
Ferriol, Marquis de: *Correspondance*, Antwerp, 1870
Herold, Ch.: *Five aspects of love*, London, 1961

Hopkinson, M. R.: *Married to Mercury*, London, 1926
Masson, P. N.: *Mme de Tencin*, Paris, 1904
La Mottraye: *Voyages . . . en Europe, Asie, Afrique*, 2 vols., London, 1727
Prévost, Abbé: *Histoire d'une Grecque Moderne*, ed. C. E. Engel, Paris, 1963
Tisseau, P.: *La Marquise de Créquy*, Paris, 1827
Tournefort, P. de: *Voyage au Levant*, Paris, 1717

CHAPTER XIII

Bertola, Abbé: *Vita del Marchese Michele Sagramoso*, Pavia, 1793
Corberon, Chevalier de: *Journal intime*, ed. Lalande, 2 vols., Paris, 1901
Engel, C. E.: *La Correspondence de J. F. de Boissy*, Neuchatel, 1941
Pierling, P.: *La Russie et le Saint Siège*, 5 vols., Paris, 1912
Riva, F.: *Il cartegio de Michele Enrico Sagramoso*, Florence, 1961
Tal hillitfor Köngliche Swensky Vetenska Academien of Herr Marquis de Sagramoso, Stockholm, 1748

CHAPTER XIV

Halsband, R.: *The Life of Lady Mary Wortley Montague*, Oxford, 1956
La Harpe, J. de: *J. P. de Crousaz*, Geneva, 1955
Quinsonnas, Chevalier F. Z. de: *Ode au roi de Prusse*; *La Capilotade*, Fontenoy, 1745; *Pièces nouvelles*, Paris, 1745
Quinsonnas, Comte de: *Monseigneur de Lauberivière*, Paris, 1936
Quinsonnas, Chevalier P. de: 'Une question de préséance au parlement de Grenoble', *Académie Delphinale*, 1912

CHAPTER XV

Daguet, A.: *Les barons de Forel*, Lausanne, 1873
Hort, P.: *La Commanderie de St Jean de Colmar*, Colmar, 1870
Meininger, E.: 'Les Commanderies de l'Ordre de St Jean de Jérusalem à Mulhouse', *Archives héraldiques Suisses*, 1924

CHAPTER XVI

Caylus, Comte de: *Recueil d'Antiquités*, 7 vols., Paris, 1752-67
Fréminville, de: 'Les Templiers de Laumusse', *Annales de la Société d'Emulation de l'Ain*, 1940
La Faveur: 'Chute d'aérolithes en Bresse en 1753', *Revue du Lyonnais*, 1880

Niepce, L.: 'Le Cabinet du Commandeur de Monts de Savasse', *Revue Lyonnaise*, 1883

Saint-Fonds, M. de, et Président Dugas: *Correspondance littéraire et anecdotique*, 2 vols., Paris, 1900

Walter, H. R.: *Catalogue of the Silver Plate at the British Museum*, London, 1921

CHAPTER XVII

Corail, R. du: *Une commanderie . . . en Charolais, Epinassy*, 1942

CHAPTER XVIII

Roland de la Platière: *Lettres écrites de Suisse . . . et de Malte*, 6 vols., Amsterdam, 1780

CHAPTER XIX

Boppe, L.: *Les peintres Français du Bosphore au XVIIIe Siècle*, Paris, 1911

Diderot, D.: *Salon de 1763*, Paris, 1876

Fosca, F.: *Liotard*, Lausanne

Houël, J.: *Voyage pittoresque de Sicile et de Malte*, 2 vols., Paris, 1787

Watelet, J.: 'L'Orient dans l'art Français', *Etudes d'Art*, 1960

CHAPTER XX

Bruun-Neergaard, F. C.: *Journal du dernier voyage du Citoyen Dolomieu dans les Alpes*, Paris, An X

Candolle, A. P. de: *Mémoires et souvenirs*, Geneva, 1862

Dolomieu, D. T. de: *Voyage aux Iles Lipari*, Paris, 1783; *Voyage dans les Iles Ponce*, Paris, 1788

Duclos, Ch.: *Voyage en Italie*, Paris, 1805

Engel, C. E.: *La Suisse et ses amis*, Neuchâtel, 1943

Freshfield, D. W.: *H. B. de Saussure*, London, 1924

Hamilton, Sir Wm.: *Campi Phlaegraei*, 3 vols., Naples, 1776

Lacroix, A.: *Notice sur Déodat de Dolomieu*, Paris, 1918; *Déodat de Dolomieu*, 2 vols., Paris, 1921

Lacépède: *Notice sur Dolomieu*, Paris, An XI

Photiadès, C.: *Les vies du comte de Cagliostro*, Paris, 1932

St Non, Abbé de: *Voyage pittoresque de Naples et de Sicile*, 6 vols., Paris, 1788

INDEX